GET OUT
OF YOUR
OWN WAY!

T0166069

GET OUT

OF YOUR OWN WAY!

How to Overcome
any Obstacle in Your Life

Larry Winget

Published 2020 by Gildan Media LLC
aka G&D Media
www.GandDmedia.com

Front cover design by David Rheinhardt of Pyrographx

Interior design by Meghan Day Healey of Story Horse, LLC

Library of Congress Cataloging-in-Publication Data is available upon request

ISBN: 978-1-7225-0233-1

10   9   8   7   6   5   4   3   2   1

Contents

Introduction

You're probably in your own way. Don't believe it? Do you talk about things that you want but don't deliver? Why is that? You're in your own way.

Get out of your way so you can actually start to accomplish the things you want. It takes more than just saying what you want. You have to actually deliver on the promises you make to yourself and to others. That's the purpose of this book: to get you unstuck from a comfortable, mediocre lifestyle and move you to where you can start to accomplish everything you'd like to have in your life.

Now I've just accused you of leading a comfortable, mediocre lifestyle, and you may respond with, "It doesn't feel that way to me." I don't care how it feels. Most people rarely move to the edge. Instead, they stay in that safe place where they're rarely challenged, where they rarely start to make the headway in their lives—personally, professionally, financially—that they'd like to make, because it's so comfortable right there in the middle.

You have to get out of that comfortable place. You have to get to that place where it's a little edgier, a little scarier, where you're challenged every single day to do more, to be more, and to have more. How do you do that? That's what this book is about.

As you go through this book with me, I want you to think about your life and what you'd really like to have happen in your life. I want you to consider all the dreams, all the hopes, all the aspirations you've ever had, and I want you to start to think about why you haven't achieved those things. I'll guarantee every single time that it's because of *you*, not because of external circumstances.

Don't whine to me about the economy, don't tell me about the government, and don't talk to me about your boss, or the fact that you were the middle child. Don't offer me any of those feeble excuses. *You're* the problem. No one else. It's up to you to start to change your life today, and that's what I'm going to show you—how you can start to change your life today by getting out of your own way.

Let me tell you what you can expect from this book. First of all, you can expect solutions. I actually think that's what you want. I think you want to read this book, then put it down and be able to start—in other words, to take action on a plan that will move you from where you are to the place you really want to be.

So let me give you some ideas. Let me give you some things that you can act upon. Let me give you some solutions to the challenges that you face. I think you want a plan. I believe you want to be able to say, "This is where I start. This is the first step. This is the second step" and ultimately reach the last step. After you've gone through those steps, you want to be able to look back and say, "Look at what I have accomplished."

That's my goal for you—to give you a plan that can move you from where you are to where you've always wanted to be. If we do that together, then we will have accomplished something. You'll be able to look back and say, "This has all been worth it."

Accomplishment, results—that's everything. I want you to have better results than you've had in the past. You do that by taking responsibility for where you are, getting together an action plan, and going to work on it. That is the purpose of this book.

Now you may be wondering why I have the right even to tell you these things. You're saying, "Who are you? Who is this guy? Why is this plan any different than any of the other plans that I've read about before? Everybody claims that they can help me move from where I am to someplace else. Why, Larry, is this any different?"

First of all, I plan to give you something that's more realistic than anything you've read before. I don't care whether you change your life or not. You're going to say, "What? A motivational guru who really doesn't care?" No, I don't, because you see, I don't live with you. I don't depend on you. My life is going to be fine without your success.

The key to changing where you are is that *you* have to care. You have to care more than I care. When you start to care more about your life than anyone else cares about it, that's when you will be willing to be brave enough to do what it takes. So I'll be honest with you, and that's different from what most of the people say: "I love you, and I want really the very best from you." I bet that's a shocker to you. I bet that's something you've never heard from anybody else who does this self-help stuff. I'm telling you right now your life is up to you. That is the cold, hard truth about success. It *is* up to you. That's how I'm different.

Another way I'm different is that I'm talking to you from a depth of experience and a depth of knowledge and research. I worked. I studied. I did research. In the last nineteen years, I've read over 4000 books. I don't know anybody who's read any more books than I have. I challenge anybody to go out there and read 4000 books on every single area of success, leadership, sales, customer service, team-work, how to get rich, how to get healthy, how to stay rich, how to stay healthy. I've actually done some research about what successful people do and the difference between unsuccessful people and successful people.

Mostly, though, I will admit that I could be the poster child for stupidity. I've made every single mistake any person could ever make in life and in business. I've screwed up my business. I've gone bankrupt financially. I grew up broke, so I started out broke, then got rich, then went bankrupt, then went from bankrupt to multimillionaire. I've screwed up my marriage. I've been a bad parent from time to time. I've delivered bad customer service. I've been a lousy boss. I've done everything in the world wrong, so everything that I teach other people to do is based on all the mistakes that I've made in my life, and on all the things that I did to overcome those mistakes, to move me to a better place.

I don't shy away from my mistakes. I don't cower down and say, "Oh, I'm a perfect guy, and I never made any mistakes." No, that's not real. I'm a real guy who screws up every single day. I've always said I do more wrong by noon than most people do in a month. It's because I do a lot of stuff.

If you're busy, and if you're taking a lot of risk, and if you're doing things that require you to take a chance, and if you're living your life and running your business to the very fullest, you're going to make mistakes. That's a good thing. You learn from those mistakes.

Maybe you have seen me on television and news shows talking about the economy, money, personal finances. I go on these shows to tell people what I've learned in my own life and what I know really works for everyone. I don't offer you some platitudes, some empty ideas. I'm offering you things that I've actually done, that I know work from my own personal experience and from that of other successful people.

Also, I don't have time for tact. I think if you're being an idiot, somebody ought to call you an idiot. If you're messing up, you ought to be told that you're messing up. There's no reason to dance around these issues. People who are doing stupid things need to be told, "This is a stupid thing. Stop doing it." In fact, you could take my whole philosophy for personal and business development and you could boil it down to this very old joke: A guy goes to a doctor and says, "Hey, doctor, it hurts when I do this." The doctor says, "Then don't do that."

That's my approach to changing your life. First of all, recognize that what you're doing is hurting you. How do you know it's hurting you? It's not creating the result that you really want. Once you know what's hurting you, stop doing it. See how simple it is?

I'm not going to sit here and tell you there are a million secrets, that there are ten ways to do this and forty-three ways to discover that. I don't believe any of that stuff. I believe success comes down to very simple things that have proven to be successful and that I've acted on to turn my life around. I'm going to give you simple, actionable ideas that you can put to use today.

You can already tell that my philosophy of self-help is different from other people's. Most people's versions of self-help focus way too much on the *help* and not nearly enough on the *self*. It's not about help. It's about self. It's about *you* taking responsibility for where you are and *you* making the decision to move from where you are to another place. It's not about me helping you. It's about you helping yourself once you have the tools to do that.

My version of self-help is also different from what you usually see, because most self-help books end up being *shelf*-help books. They sit on the shelf, and they never get used. You probably have great self-help books right now in your library, and they're just sitting there. They hit you when you saw them at the bookstore, and you said, "I probably should read that." Then you took it home, and it sat on your bookshelf. Why? Because it wasn't important enough for you to make the change. If it's important for you to make the change, then you will pull those books off the shelf, and you will start using them.

I want that to happen with this book because I believe you can read it, see the simplicity of my message, and say, "This is actually something I can do." If you believe you can really do it, that's when you will start to make amazing changes in your life.

My principles are very simple. In fact, I really only have five basic principles to live your life by.

1. Your life is your own damn fault. Now that may bother you, but I promise you that's true. You created it. It was your thoughts, your words, your actions that created the results that you're experiencing today. Nobody else did that to you. Even if by chance something horrible befell you, the way you reacted to that thing, the way you responded to that circumstance—that's still your fault.

2. You have to take responsibility for your life.
    It's your fault; take responsibility for it. Own
    it. Don't start blaming other people. Don't
    whine about the fact that you have problems.
    We all have problems. It doesn't matter that
    you have problems; it's what you do about
    them. Take responsibility. Take ownership of
    your situation. Go to the mirror, look yourself
    in the eye, and say, "I created this." That's
    hard for some people to do, but once you know
    that you've created your own life through
    your thoughts, your words, your actions, and
    you stop making excuses, you're taking the
    first step in turning your life around.

3. Once you've taken responsibility, once you
    know that your actions, your thoughts, your
    words created the mess you're in, then you
    need to learn whatever it takes to fix it. You
    have to get some education. Learn what you
    need to do to fix your situation.

    The good news is, there's a lot of infor-
    mation out there. There are a lot of books,
    a lot of great lectures and seminars. There
    are even some great television programs that
    you can tune into. There's great information
    out there, but you have to be willing to read,

watch, experience it so you can learn what it takes to fix your situation.

4. You have to take action on what you've just learned. It's not enough just to know it. You have to go to work, you have to apply the information. That's where it all falls apart. People don't take action. They don't go to work. They have the knowledge. Big deal. Knowledge alone won't fix anything. People say knowledge is power. No, it's not. Knowledge is *not* power. It's the implementation of knowledge that is power. You need to implement the knowledge that you have. You have to go to work on it.

5. You have to enjoy the results. What good would it do to make all this money, to become successful, become incredibly healthy, and do what it takes to have a great relationship with everyone in your life, to lose weight, and look great? What good would it do to have all those things and then not know how to enjoy them?

Larry's Five Principles

1. Your life is your own damn fault.

2. You have to take responsibility for your life.

3. Learn what you need to do fix your situation.

4. Take action on what you've learned.

5. Enjoy the results that you've created.

Why is my approach more important than ever? Why do we need to look at what it takes to move you from where you are to a better place? Why do I keep harping on the idea that you have to take responsibility? Because it has never been more important. Right now we live in a society of victims. We want to blame everyone for our situation. We want everyone else to come to the rescue. We have this sense of entitlement, believing that when a problem happens to us, it's up to someone else to fix it for us, because how could it possibly be our fault? It doesn't matter whether we ever had the money to buy a house. We bought the house whether we could afford it or not, and now that we can't afford it, we want someone to come in and bail us out. We want someone else to come to the rescue.

We're all looking for the Lone Ranger, who will ride up on his white horse and say, "Don't worry. I'll fix this." That's not going to happen. We have to understand now more than ever that if we want to get ahead, no one is going to come to the rescue, nor should they. You have to rescue yourself. It's up to you.

Why should you fix it? One, because you can. Two, because you have obligations. Three, because you have people you are responsible for. Even if you don't have a spouse or family, you have *you*. You are responsible for your life. As responsible human beings who create the lives we have, it is up to us to keep our word, to do the right thing, to live lives of integrity and honesty and openness. We need to be responsible for every action that we have taken, whether we understood it or not at the time. It doesn't matter. We created the life we have, and it's up to us to maintain that life, because we said we would. We gave our word. We need to stop being victims and start being in control of our lives.

Too many people in society complain that they have no control. There *are* a lot of things you don't have any control over. You have no control over what groceries cost. You have no control over what gasoline costs—none. Don't worry about it; you can't do anything about it. If it went to $15 a gallon, all you could do is sit on your butt, not drive your car, and whine about it. How much good would that do? The only things you can do are the things within your own control, the things you have power over. I want you to stop worrying about everything you can't control and start being concerned about what you *can* control.

You can control your life. You can control your own level of consumption. You can control how much you spend, how deep in debt you go, how much you weigh, how much you exercise, pretty much how healthy you are. You control your relationships. You can control how much time you spend with people. You can control the level of energy you put into something. All of those things are within your control.

Take control of the things you can control, that you can handle, that you can manage, and let go of the things you can't. When you do that, I promise you: that action alone—becoming responsible for the things you can control—will turn your life around forever. You will see amazing changes.

Right now, more than ever, we need to start taking control of our lives, and that's what I want to teach you how to do in this book. First of all, though, I want to show you how ridiculous all of us are when it comes to taking control of our lives. We are out of control. We do stupid things. I'm astounded at the stupid things we do in so many areas of our lives.

Let's start off with health. Do you ever want to see an area where people are going to lie to you? It's when they say they want to be healthy. We hear people every day on television saying, "I want to be healthy." Do you really? How do your actions back that up? They don't. We just say we want to be healthy.

Life is short. Ever said that? Sure you have. We all know life is short, and yet why do we, every single day, do things to make sure that life will actually be shorter than it has to be?

Do you know that over 300,000 adults are going to die in the United States every year because of their own unhealthy eating habits, because of their sedentary behavior, because they're inactive? Only about 23 percent of Americans get the recommended amount of exercise per week.

We live sedentary lifestyles. We'd rather watch people on television lose weight than get up off the couch and do what it takes to lose weight ourselves. We're spectators. We're not involved. We're not active in life. We say we want to be healthy, yet we don't do the things it takes to get healthy. In 2017, we spent $66 billion on weight-loss products and services, but all it would really take would be to eat a little less and go for a walk. Just do that. You'll see amazing results in your weight if you just eat less and exercise more. Is it that simple? Yeah, pretty much.

The other day I read a review of one of my books, and it said, "I don't know how in the world this guy could be a guru to anyone about anything. He doesn't seem all that bright to me." Then it said, "This guy actually thinks that in order to weigh less, pretty much all you have to do is eat less and exercise more." Yeah, that's really pretty much all it takes. The reviewer went on to say, "This guy also believes that in order to have more money, all you have to do is earn more money or spend less of the money you have." Again, yeah. You see, we want hard solutions. I don't give you hard solutions.

Let me point out some ridiculous behavior and show you that small, simple changes in your behavior can create amazing results.

People say they want to live long, healthy lives. Oh, yeah? Do you know that there 1.1 billion smokers in the world today? Do you know that every cigarette you smoke shortens you life by thirteen minutes? Think of all the fun you could have in thirteen minutes. So why do you kill yourself by choice?

Every day people choose to do things that shorten their lives. The daily caloric intake of the average American is more than 3,300 calories. That's a third more than anybody ought to eat. The average American only needs 2,500 calories. The average female only needs 1,900 calories. Doctors will back it up: 90 percent of obesity is directly related to lifestyle. If you want to change your life, change your lifestyle. Exercise more, eat less.

If this is true for you, do you see how you're getting in your own way here?

More proof that people do stupid things: People say that they want to have great kids. Don't you want to have great kids? If you're a parent, of course you want to have great kids. I could go out to any parent on the street and say, "What's important to you?" and they would say, "My kids are important to me."

Yet the most recent study said that the average parent in America only spends three and a half minutes per week in meaningful conversation with their children. Three and a half minutes per week, 210 seconds, thirty seconds a day. Oh, you bet. We want to have good kids. Obviously not enough to talk to them.

We don't back up what we say we want with our actions. It's easy to say you want good kids. How much time are you spending communicating with your kids? How much time do you spend playing with your kids?

People say they want to have great schools for their kids. We want good public schools. Yet only a very small percentage of parents belong to or attend the PTA meetings that the schools put on. They're not involved in their kids' lives. Do you know that 25 percent of all teenage girls right now in the United States have STDs? Come on, parents. Where are you? If 25 percent of girls have STDs, there's something wrong. Don't tell me you want great kids while you're doing very little to make sure you actually have great kids.

Health and kids are a great place to show you how stupid we all are when I comes to our parenting. Nineteen percent of children two to nineteen years old are overweight. Don't blame anyone but yourself as a parent on this one. You buy the groceries, you cook the food, and you put it in front of them, or you take them to a place and buy them food. We need to start caring for our kids, and we need to care enough about our kids to feed them healthy food. We have an obese society. If your kid is at obese at the age of eighteen, in all likelihood that kid will be an obese adult, and their life will end sooner than it has to.

Get control of your kids. Take control by talking to them, communicating with them, disciplining them, playing with them, having fun with them, going to their school, going to their activities, and feeding them in healthy ways.

How about finances? People sign a deal with a credit-card company. They sign their name. They sign their name on their mortgage. They sign their name on all kinds of loan documents. Then somewhere along the way, they forget that signing your name is a legally binding contract. In that contract, you say you will make a certain payment on a certain day of the month. Then it becomes inconvenient for you.

I'm sorry. It doesn't matter whether it's inconvenient. It doesn't matter whether something else came up or not. You made a deal, and a deal is a deal. You signed a legally binding contract that says you will make this payment on this day of the month. When you don't, don't be surprised when they trash your credit for not keeping your word. They kept *their* word. Don't be surprised when they call you and say, "Where's my money?" It's their money. They fronted you that money. They have every right to ask for it.

People wreck their credit because it has become inconvenient to pay their bills on time. I'm sorry, but when it comes to giving your word financially, you do what you said you would do. Period. It doesn't matter whether it's convenient. It doesn't matter whether they were having a shoe sale, and you just had to spend your money because those shoes wouldn't be on sale ever again, and you needed to buy them instead of making your credit-card payment. Those things don't matter. You have to keep your word when it comes to your finances.

As long as we're on credit cards, don't have more than three credit cards. You don't need a big stack of credit cards. You need something that you can control, and you can only control about three.

In fact, you can move from where you are to a better place very simply in the area of money. I'm going to talk a lot more about in this book because if there's ever an area of life where you can get control and start to see a major difference very quickly, it's money.

Let me give you another example to show where we're stupid when it comes to our money. Did you realize that the average fifty-year-old in America has less than $2,500 in cash saved? Let me do a little math for you. Let's say you went to work when you're twenty-five years old. Now it's twenty-five years later. You're fifty years old, and the best you could do was save $2,500—$100 a year, $8.33 a month, less than $2 a week? Come on. That's stupid.

If you only have $2,500 to your name when you're fifty years old, what kind of person are you? You're a person who never made it a priority to have a financially secure future. If you had, you would have put some money away.

Instead people would rather just say, "The economy sucks, and nobody has any money." That's not true. People have money because they choose to have money. People pay their bills because they choose to pay their bills. People have great kids because that's been their choice. Every single area of life—it doesn't matter what it is—comes down to the choices that you've made.

Remember, life is your own damn fault, and the choices you make, those are your fault, and the results that you're experiencing, those are your fault. When you start to make better choices, you will create better results. That's what you want, isn't it, better results?

Make better choices. That's the process for getting great results. You do that in the area of money; you do that in the area of your health. All of these come down to making good choices. If this is true, do you see how you're sabotaging yourself? Start with the end in mind. Realize what you want your kids to look like when they're thirty-five years old. Look at how you want your finances to be when you're fifty or sixty or sixty-five. How do you want your life to look? How healthy do you want to be down the road? Then work backwards and do whatever it takes to make that happen. All this stuff really is very simple.

So far I've talked to you about your health and your money and your kids. But you can think of lots of other areas where people do stupid things. Let me give you some examples from business. People say they want customers, yet they don't treat the customers very well. You can go into a business, and you'll be hard-pressed to get greeted at the door. You'll be hard-pressed to go to a cash register and pay for your item and even have the clerk look at you and acknowledge your presence, much less count any change or thank you for shopping here. They're either on their cell phone or they're talking to their coworkers. We want customers—just not enough to treat them well, not enough to greet them, appreciate their presence, or say thank-you for shopping with us.

I get emails every day from people who have started businesses, and then they're in trouble. I always ask, "What did you do to prepare yourself to go into business?"

"I was passionate, Larry. I had a great passion for embroidering pillows and selling them on the Internet." Really? How's that passion thing paying out for you? Why didn't you study what it takes to set a business up, how to set up a payroll, how to deal with suppliers, how to treat customers, how to market, how to sell? It takes more than passion to be successful in business. It takes business ethics. It takes business skills. You have to prepare yourself before you start out in business.

Business is an amazing area where people do stupid things. They go to work late, they take long lunch hours, or they slip out on sales calls and get a haircut or go shopping. Then they wonder why they were laid off. They ought to feel fortunate that they weren't fired a long time ago, because they probably weren't working hard enough to have the right to keep their job to begin with. People work just hard enough not to get fired. They wonder why they don't get the raise, they don't get the promotion, or they're the first person let go when times get tough. It's because they're not working very hard.

I read a study the other day that was done among American workers. They were asked, "How much of the time you spend on the job is actually spent working?" Amazingly, the answer was about half. About half the time we spend on the job is actually spent doing the job, and now we wonder how we're able to keep a business alive during a tough economic time with half as many employees. It's because people are only working half the time to begin with. So if you have 100 percent of the employees working half the time, all you have to do is get rid of half of them and make sure that the half you keep work 100 percent of the time. That's how simple this really is.

Let's look at more idiotic behavior, and you can have some fun with this one yourself. (In fact, you'll probably think of a lot more than I'm giving you here.) Have you ever been at the drive-in bank, and you're sitting in a line of four or five cars, and finally you're the next car? The car in front of you pulls up to the window, and you see the driver start to fill out the deposit slip or start to count the money they want to put in the bank. You see them do all their paperwork. They've been in line for four or five cars, and they haven't done a darn thing except sit there. Now it's their turn, and they get busy.

Does it drive you crazy? It drives me crazy. It's because people aren't paying attention. They do stupid things, they don't take responsibility for their own time, and they're discourteous to other people and don't respect their time. We have to stop doing stupid things.

Let me give you some more examples. People get drunk and drive and then sue the bartender or the bar. But they were the ones buying the drinks and drinking the drinks! People say they want to have a great relationship with their spouse, yet a recent study says that 65 percent of people spend more time on their computers than they do with their spouses. We spend more time with our computers than we do with the person that we say that we love the most in the whole world. Then we wonder why our relationships are falling apart.

People with no job and nothing but time on their hands have the dirtiest cars, the filthiest houses, and the most overgrown yards. How is that? They have all the time in the world. They could pick up around the house. They could take a hose and wash their own car. They could mow their yard. Do they? No, because they're lazy. That's probably why they don't have a job.

The average American reads at a seventh-grade level. You would think that a country that claims to be the biggest, brightest, and best country on the planet could turn out smarter people, wouldn't you? The truth is, we're not the brightest. We don't rank number one in anything in the world except consumerism. Our students are well below all international averages in terms of math and science, and 40 percent of high-school students haven't mastered what they need at any grade level. We turn out kids and hand them high-school diplomas, and some of them can't even read their own diplomas.

How about this? The human race, knowingly, every single day, is destroying the environment. You know we are. I'm not a huge environmentalist, but I think that we have to take responsibility for our planet and start to do things that make sense for it.

Then too, every year people spend millions of dollars on psychics. Come on—psychics? No one can predict your future except you, and you do that by taking control of your future. So stop spending money with these frauds.

This one hits me a lot: people want advice. People beg for advice. I get a hundred emails a day from people begging me to help them with their problem, whether it be a money problem or a business problem or they've just gotten laid off. "Larry, give me some advice."

You know what's amazing when people ask you for advice? Very few of them take the advice. In fact, many of them will argue with you when you give them the advice. This is a person who doesn't have any money, doesn't have a job, has made nothing but mistakes in their life. They ask you what they ought to do. You tell them what they ought to do, and they say, "You know, I don't think that will work."

Don't ask me then. No wonder you're in a mess. You're not willing to take any advice. You're too hardheaded to listen to somebody who actually knows what they're talking about.

The point is this. Stop doing what's hurting you. Stop doing whatever is keeping you from achieving your goals. Figure out what is not giving you the results that you want, and stop doing those things. Only at that point can you start to do the things that do create the life that you want.

All right. Now let me give you the clincher, the biggest proof of all that we all do stupid things every single day. Human beings are the only species on earth who knowingly choose to be less, do less, and have less than they could.

Nothing else on our planet does that. No other living creature does that. Only people do that. You dog doesn't do that. Plants don't do that. Plants don't grow to a certain level and just go, "Eh, I'm good," and stop. That's not how plants grow. That's not how any other creature grows. Only people choose to have less, be less, and do less than they could. That ought to upset you. You, every single day, choose to do less than you know you could. You choose to have less than you could, and you choose to be less than you could. Why? It's because you're willing to accept the results that you have. Do you see how you're getting in your own way here?

I often start off my sessions by asking the audience, "How many of you are 100 percent satisfied with every single area of your life? I mean, you like how much you weigh. You like how much money you have in the bank. You like your situation with your spouse. You love the relationship you have with your kids or with your own parents. Every single thing about your life, you love it all just exactly the way it is." Then I ask for a show of hands. I never get any hands on that, because no one wants to say that they love every single area of life the way it is.

Then I say, "You're liars. You are satisfied with your lives exactly the way it is. You like your relationships the way they are. You like how much you weigh. You like how much money you have in the bank. No? I'm right, because if you didn't like it, it would be different. Your life is the way it is because that's how you choose it to be, and you're willing to accept it just the way it is. Otherwise it would be different."

If you're finally fed up with your life the way it is right now, and you're really willing to make a change, this is the time to do it. This is the time to start taking responsibility for where you are—opening yourself up to some new, simple ideas that you can take action on to create the life you want.

Before moving forward, the key is, first of all, to admit that you are sabotaging yourself. Once you realize that it's *you* that is in the way of your success, it's *you* that has gotten in the way of you having more, being more, that's when you're ready to move forward. If you haven't done that yet, stop and realize your mistakes, stop and realize your successes, stop and take account of where you are in your life, and then take responsibility for the choices that you've made. When you realize that you have made mistakes and you're willing to be responsible for those mistakes, that's when you're able to move forward and start to fix them.

I had to do that in every single area of my life. I told you: I could have been the poster child for stupidity. I have messed up every single area of my life, and first of all I had to take responsibility for that.

I know this is hard. I know I'm asking you to make a major shift in the way you think. But to be successful in life, be healthy, have more money, have great relationships, you have to be tuned into who you are and what you really want. It is difficult, but if life is hard, why do you make it harder than it has to be? Why are you in your own way? Why don't you get out of your way and start tackling life's challenges so you can get on top of things, start to make changes, and—maybe for the first time ever—be in true control of your life?

Are you ready to do that? If you are, let's start looking at the ways in which we sabotage our lives.

The Power of Lists

'm a big believer in lists. I think people ought to write things down. I believe in working from documents, not just from thought. So at some point you will need to get out a sheet of paper and a pen and start to actually write things down. Later I'm going to show you how to take action on these items and come up with a plan.

Born Ignorant

Let me start with the number-one way we sabotage ourselves: ignorance. We're ignorant. You may say, "That's very harsh." No, it's not. Ignorance simply means that you don't know what it takes. You don't have the information. You are ignorant of what it takes to do better or to have more or to be more successful.

We're all born ignorant. When you're born, you're a blank slate, and along the way you learn everything that you need to survive. You learn that when you fall down, it hurts, so you'd better figure out how to walk so you don't fall down all the time. You learn that when you touch something that's hot, it hurts, so you learn not to touch something that's hot. We learn through experience. We learn through people talking to us and teaching us. We learn in lots of different ways, and yet there's so much in life that we remain ignorant of.

If you don't know how to play golf, if you're ignorant of how to play golf, that's really not a big deal. There was a time in my life I didn't have a clue about how to play golf. I did finally learn how. I'm not very good at it, but at least I learned the basics. There was a time in my life when I sat down at a big dinner table at a banquet and I didn't know which fork to use or which side my bread plate was on. Is that any huge deal? No, it's a little bit embarrassing from time to time, but it's not a life-and-death situation. We all have things that it's OK to be ignorant about, because they're not life-and-death situations.

But when it comes to what it takes to be successful, to be healthy, to be financially secure, it is absolutely inexcusable to be ignorant about those things.

Don't come to me with the excuse, "No one ever taught me." That's fine until you're about thirteen. At about thirteen, if you don't know how to be successful, or you don't know how to be healthy, or you don't know what it takes to be financially secure, you'd better get a book. You'd better start asking questions. You'd better pay more attention in class. You'd better do whatever it takes on your own, because you're not getting it at home. You need to go out and seek out the knowledge about what it takes to be healthy, financially secure, and successful. You cannot afford to be ignorant about those three things.

Are there things in your life that you've been ignorant about? Are there things that you don't have information about, that you need to know, in order to be healthy, more successful, or financially secure? Make a list right now. Write down some things that you know that you just don't have the information about.

Do you need to learn how to budget better, how to save, how to invest your money? Write that down. Do you need to know how to get on a health program, what exercises you should be doing, what foods would be more nutritious? Do you need to know what it takes to be more successful in your job, to do better when you go to work, to get along better with your spouse or with your kids, to be a better parent? Do you need to know those things? Make that list now.

The Meaning of Stupidity

Now let's move to the second way we sabotage our lives: we're stupid.

You're saying, "How dare you say that I'm stupid?" Let me explain myself. First of all, we start out not having the information. That's ignorance. But when you get the information and don't do anything with it, that's stupid. How could you have information about what it takes to be more successful, healthier, financially secure, a better parent, a better spouse, and not use it? The only answer is that you're stupid. So you have to move beyond stupidity.

Now everybody knows something about what it takes to be more successful in life. I've already pointed out how simple it is to weigh less: you eat less and exercise more. It really is that simple. That may not be everything you need to know in your particular situation; there are always some exceptions. But I don't deal much with exceptions, because most people like to think they are exceptions when they're not. That idea—eat less, exercise more—will work for just about everybody on the planet. It's not everything you need to know, but it's enough for you to get started.

You want to be more financially secure. You know that you probably need to spend less money. You probably need to save more money. You probably need to adjust your lifestyle when things are hard. You know these things. They're not everything you need to know to be financially secure, but they're enough for you to get started.

You want to have better kids. Without reading a book, you know exactly what you ought to do to have better kids. You ought to spend more time with them. You ought to tuck them in at night and ask them how their day was. You ought to cook them a great meal and sit down with them and enjoy that meal. You know what it takes.

We all know what it takes to be in better relationships. We know what it takes to be smarter: read a book. We know what it takes in every area of life. We all have enough information to get started.

So we're really not completely ignorant in any area. We have some information. The problem is that we don't do what it takes to implement that information.

Here's what I want you to do. I want you to make a list of all the areas where you know you have the information and you aren't doing anything with it.

Do you weigh too much? You know what it takes. Write that down. Are you not taking advantage of all the intelligence that you have when it comes to getting ahead at work? Write that down.

Do you know that you ought to be spending more time with your spouse, maybe taking them on a date once a week, or tucking your kids in at night, or maybe cooking better for them at home instead of doing the easy thing and buying them hamburgers at a fast-food joint? You know those things, and you're not doing them. Write them down.

Take a moment, get honest with yourself, and think of the areas in your life where you know what it takes to do better, to have more, to be more successful, and write those things down.

Moving beyond Laziness

All right. If you know what it takes to be successful, if you have that information, and you're not doing anything with it, why not? My guess is because you're lazy.

I know that hurts. You're probably saying, "Oh, Larry, you don't understand. I'm a busy person. I have more going on. I have a long drive to get to work. It takes me a while to get there, and then by the time I get there, I have to stand around and get a cup of coffee, and then I have to go to my desk, or I have to get busy doing things, and I'm busy all day long. By the time I come home, I have to cook dinner. I have to sit back and watch a little TV and relax, and then I have to mess with the kids, and then shoot, Larry, I have to take a shower and go to bed."

Welcome to life. You're busy. Everybody's busy. I never met anybody who wasn't busy. The point is, what are you busy doing? Are you busy doing things that move you closer to where you want to be, or are you doing things that don't really matter?

That really is the key: whether you're doing things that move you closer to your goals or things that really aren't all that important. You know that if you read a book about business success, it would have at least one little piece of information that you could take away and use. You could implement that idea, and you would see a positive change in your life. You know that.

However, you also know it's Monday night, and *Monday Night Football* is on, and you just can't miss that. Maybe while you're watching that rerun of *Seinfeld* that you've seen all those times, and you can almost say the words with them, your little kid comes up and says, "Daddy, could you help me? I have to study for my spelling bee."

You go, "What, and miss this? This is really funny, honey. Crawl up here on Daddy's lap." So she doesn't study for the test, and you end up watching television that you've seen before, and it's not done anybody any good.

It's not that we don't have time. It's that we don't have time for the things that are really important. There's always enough time to do what's really important, but we get caught up doing things that aren't important.

Do you realize that the average person watches television six hours a day? If you watch television six hours a day, then you're lazy, especially if you do it at the sacrifice of something that really does matter. Add a computer to that mix, and typically there's another hour and a half per day that gets wasted. You add a video game; for some people, that's another hour and a half. That's eight or nine hours per day in the average household that is spent being entertained, being a spectator of life instead of becoming involved in life. You're doing things that don't move you closer to where you want to be.

It's easier to watch *Friends* on TV than it is to get up off our butts and go find a friend, be a friend, or have a friend. It's easier to watch people get a job on television than it is to update our résumé and study a little to be qualified for a better job. It's easier to watch people lose weight on television than to get up and go for a walk, do a little exercise, create a healthy meal instead of eating the fast stuff, which has no nutritional value. It's easier to watch somebody raise their kids on television than it is for us to get up and take the action, spend the time, and do what's necessary to make sure that we're raising our own kids.

Why don't we do those things? They're not important to us. They're not important enough for us to put our time and our energy into. You have to decide in which areas of your life you are being lazy, and you have to stop right now.

Stop and make a list of the areas in your life where you know that you've been less than active, where you've been a spectator, where you've let things slide and you shouldn't have. Be honest with yourself and make that list. Don't be lazy and skip it.

These are the first three ways you're sabotaging your life: ignorance, stupidity, and laziness. Let's really get ugly now.

Not Giving a Damn

The fourth way we sabotage our lives is just by not giving a damn. It's true. You don't care. You don't care enough to do whatever it takes. You say, "But

I do care." Do you really? I've already pointed out how we say we care about our kids, yet we don't do the things that prove it. I've shown you that the way to be healthy, and yet we don't follow it. We say we care about those things. I don't buy it.

You need to understand this: your time, your energy, and your money always go to what really is important to you. That's how you'll spend your money. All you have to do is track your money to find out what you really give a damn about. Spend a few minutes with your checkbook. Look at your credit-card statement. Walk through your house. See how you're spending your money. You know what you give a damn about? You give a damn about the things that you're spending your money on.

Where do you put your energy? How do you spend your time? Track your time for a day. If you'll track your time for a day, you'll find out very quickly what's really important to you and who's really important to you.

If all of your time is spent on the job, then your job is the most important thing to you. If all of your time is spent watching television, then television is the most important thing to you. If you're balanced, and you spend time at work, time at play, time exercising, and time with your family, it's because balance is important to you. It all comes down to priorities. You can always track a person's money, energy, and time to figure out what their priorities really are. Life is pretty much like a crime novel. Just follow the money, and you'll find what's caused the biggest problems in your life. If looking cute is important to you, you'll spend your money at the mall. If being cool is important to you, you'll probably drive a fancy car or have a sixty-inch plasma TV hanging on the wall. That's not a problem: you can have all those things as long as you can afford them. If you can't, but you spend your money on them anyway, then your priorities are out of whack.

Look at other areas. You say you want to be successful. Really? How much time are you spending studying success? How many books like this are you reading? It doesn't seem that success is all that important to you if you're not doing what it takes to be more successful in your mind and your body and your work. You're not really preparing yourself for success.

If you eat like a pig, and you end up looking like a pig, and you don't care anything about your health, I'm telling you that you don't really care that much about your family. "Larry, that's not fair." Of course it's fair. If you cared about your family, you would do everything within your power to stay healthy so that you could live a long time. Then you could be with your family, spend time with them, provide for them, enjoy them.

Don't tell me that your family is important to you. Don't tell me that your kids are important to you when you're do everything in the world to contradict yourself and end your life sooner than you have to. Or when you're not making as much money as you could in order to provide for them in the best possible way. If your family really is that meaningful to you, you'll do all of those things, because you want the best for them.

You know that if you smoke, you're going to die sooner than you would if you didn't smoke. Then you must not give a damn about living. Oh, that hurts, doesn't it? Welcome to the truth. Sometimes the truth hurts; that's how you know it's the truth. The truth is ugly. It hurts sometimes, and that's why you need to hear it. In fact, I believe if somebody says something really nice to you, they're probably lying to you.

Let me see if I can hurt you a little more with some truth. If you choose to watch television instead of reading a book that might help you get a better job, then you don't give a damn about providing for your family to the best of your ability.

If you don't give your job your very best every minute that you're there, then you don't give a damn about your job. You also don't give a damn about keeping your word, because when you went to work for them, you said that you would work hard, you would give it your best every single day, and you're not doing it. That makes you a liar and a thief. You're stealing from your employer.

If you don't pay your bills on time, then you lack integrity. You don't care about keeping your word, because you said you would pay your bills when you took out the credit card, when you bought the house, when you bought the car. You said you would pay your bills on time, and now you're not. It must not be all that important to you. If you don't vote in the next election, you don't give a damn about the direction our country is going in. If you don't take the time to tell or show your spouse you love her, then you must not give a damn about her. If you're like the average fifty-year-old in America with less than $2,500 saved, you don't give a damn about your retirement, or about your kids going to college.

You may be saying, "But Larry, that's not fair." Of course it's fair. Even if it's not, who promised you fairness in life? There are no guarantees of fairness in life.

You can argue about this, but it's black-and-white. Stop rationalizing your less than intelligent behavior, and stop trying to find a gray area into which you can fit all the compromises that you made with yourself. You have to start taking responsibility for your actions. There are no gray areas in life. It really is black-and-white. You have to start backing up what you say you give a damn about with your actions. If you don't put your time in it, you don't care about it. If you don't put any energy toward it, you don't care about it. If you don't spend your money on it, then you don't care about it.

I want you to make a list of all the things you believe you care about. Write down your family. Write down your health. Write down your career.

Once you've done that, I want you to make a list of all the things you care about *based on the evidence.* The evidence is your bank statement. The way you've spent your time over the course of a week. Walking through your house and looking at the things you spent your money on. The evidence is what you do when you get home from work, or the people that you hang around. This second list is the evidence of what you really care about based on how you spend your time, where you put your energy, and how you spend your money.

When you come up with that list, compare it with the first one. Chances are, they'll be different. You might realize then that you've been lying to yourself.

You said certain things were important to you, but the evidence simply doesn't prove it.

You need to change. You need to change the way you spend your time, you need to change the way you spend your money, and you need to change the way your energy is spent as well. You need to look at what you really say is important to you in life and back it up with your actions, with your words, with your thoughts, your energy, and your money.

Sadly, though, people rarely make a change until it's nearly too late. You've seen it so many times; I know you have. We wait until it's just almost too late to fix things, to start realizing what we really care about. People say they want to stop smoking. Sadly, most people stop smoking when they're diagnosed with emphysema or lung cancer. That's when they're really serious about it. Once they've been told they're going to die from smoking, they'll cover their body in patches and pray that they never pick up another pack. Most people don't quit smoking until it's almost too late.

When do people finally decide, "Boy, I better get serious and start exercising and stop eating so much"? When they have a heart attack, when they've been diagnosed with diabetes, when their cholesterol is off the charts. That's when they get serious—when it's almost too late.

When do people get really concerned about going to work and actually working? When layoffs are in the air, when the boss comes down and says, "We need to see productivity go way up, or we're going to have to shut this place down." Boy, people get concerned about working then. The problem is it's almost too late. It's hard to pull it out of the fire when you've almost lost your company, your job. You should have been more concerned about that along the way.

I don't want it to be too late for you, and I know you don't want it to be too late. I want you to get in control of your life right now. I want you to look at these lists that you've just made, and I want you to say what's really important to you, not based on your words alone, but based on your actions.

Then I want you to discover your priorities and back them up with your actions. Prove to yourself and everyone else that they're important to you by putting your thoughts, your words, your actions, your time, your energy, and your money into them. That's when they will become real priorities, and the results will be the way you want them to be.

2

Move Past
Self-Sabotage!

Let me ask you about those lists. Are you actually doing them, or are you going to sabotage your future more by not doing the one thing that I think will make one of the biggest differences in your future—actually putting your thoughts, your plans, your ideas down on paper?

You have to be willing to do that in order to see real results in your life. I'm not going to let you off the hook on this. I want to make sure that when you finish this book, you will have a stack of paper in front of you on which you've been honest with yourself and have created the life that you'd like to have. You'll have a hard, actionable plan in front of you that you can refer to, so keep after those lists.

Vision, Right and Wrong

Now let's look at the next way we sabotage ourselves. We don't have vision. Sometimes the vision that we do have is the wrong vision. In fact, one reason people aren't successful is that they can't create the kind of vision they'd like to have for their lives. They're stuck seeing life exactly the way it is right now and the way it has been instead of the way it could be.

You have to move beyond that vision of the way your life has always looked and begin to picture your life the way you want it to look. If I hadn't done that, I'd still be living in the little town of Muskogee, Oklahoma, making very little money, like the rest of my family, living a mediocre, safe, little life. I'd probably have been working for a big company, had a nice, little house on a nice, little street in the nice, little town where I'd grown up.

If I hadn't changed my vision for my life, that would be the kind of life I'm living today, but I always had a bigger vision for my life. I saw it unfolding in ways that nobody I'd been around could ever imagine.

When I was thirteen years old, I was humiliated over the fact that I didn't have money. A kid made fun of me for only having one pair of jeans. At that point I decided to get a new vision for my life, because I refused to be humiliated ever again for growing up broke. I saw myself as being rich. I didn't know what that really looked like except when my parents put me in the car, we drove to other side of town, where the rich folks lived, and I got to see their houses. I knew that even though I didn't know how that was going to happen for me, I had to start to be able to picture that as my life.

I could picture myself living in one of the big houses instead of the little World War I barracks that my dad had converted to our home. I would own a house where people would walk in and say, "Wow." I would have a closet full of cool clothes, and I'd have lots of watches and cool jewelry, and I'd live like a millionaire.

When I started in professional speaking, I had the audacity to see myself as a huge success. I saw myself on stages with tens of thousands of people in the audience, laughing at every joke that came out of my mouth, writing down every intelligent word that I said. I saw myself on television, being interviewed by some of the biggest people in the business. When I started writing books, I could see the titles of my books and my name at the top of *The New York Times* and *The Wall Street Journal* best-seller lists.

I had those pictures in my mind, and I held on to them. And you know what? Every single one of those things happened. I'm fortunate that, through my hard work and my vision and my plan for my life, I've actually been able to create all of those things. I have written best-selling books, and I've been interviewed by some of the biggest people in the entertainment and news industries. I do live in a house in which I get up every morning and go, "Wow." I dress a little strange for a lot of people, but it's the way I like to dress based on my personal vision of success.

How was I able to do that? I created the vision in my mind. I held that vision in my mind every single day. That was my end result. It's what I pictured. It's what I worked toward. It's the picture I had in my mind; every single morning when I woke up, that was the first thing I could see. It moved from where I could see it to where I could feel it. It moved from where I could see it and feel it to where I believed that I could make it happen, if—and it's a big *if*—I was willing to work hard enough, if I created a plan that I could work on every single day to make it happen.

Here's the good news for you. You can create a new vision for your life. I don't care what your life looks like right now. Don't write and tell me how bad it is. Don't even tell yourself how bad it is. I get sick of people writing me and whining about how bad it is. Who cares how bad it is right now? How do you *want* it to be? We spend so much time and energy wallowing in the pain of how it is today instead of creating a vision of how we would like it to be in our lives and working hard enough to make that vision take place.

You don't have to live with the vision that you have right now. You're not stuck with it. Nobody is standing there holding a gun to your head saying, "Think that way forever and ever and ever and ever." No, you can change that quickly. You can dump everything that you've been thinking, snap your fingers, and make a new decision. You can create a new vision for your life. You can erase the picture you have in your mind and create a whole new picture. All it takes is some imagination, a belief that you have the ability to do this, based on how hard you're willing to work. You weren't just dealt this hand of cards and stuck with them. I know that sounds wrong, because everybody says, "That's just the hand I was dealt." Throw that hand back. Demand a redeal. You can do that. If life won't give you a redeal, jerk the cards out of its hands and deal yourself a new hand. You have that power.

I get sick of people saying stupid stuff like, "Well, it is what it is." No, it isn't. It is the way I *allow* it to be. You need to say that, because it is the way you allow it to be, and it's the way it is because that's what you're willing to accept.

How about this one? I know you've heard this. The most idiotic, depressing, self-defeating song in the history of our society—"Que Sera, Sera." Remember that? "The future's not ours to see." The future *is* yours to see. The future *is* yours to create. You don't have to accept things the way they are. You can turn your back on your past. You can turn your back on every vision you've ever been forced to look at, every vision that you've decided is OK. Every way your life is doesn't mean that your life has to be that way in the future. You can choose a new vision for your life.

What does the vision you have for your life look like right now? Not sure? Let me help you with this. You're living the vision you have for your life. Everything that's going on in your life right now, everything that you're experiencing, you are experiencing because of the vision you have for your life. The house you live in is the vision you have. The relationship that you're in right now is the vision you have for the relationships you were willing to be in. The money in your wallet is your vision for how much money you believe that you deserve. That's how it works.

Your life is the way you want it to be. It's the way you want it to be because that's what you're willing to accept. That's the vision you're willing to have. Refuse to accept that, and create a new vision for your life. If you don't like how your life looks, and if this is how it looks, then change the way it looks. You can do that.

Here's what I want you to do. I want you to write down a new vision for your life. Forget the way it is. I don't want you to think about reality right now. I want you to write down the vision you have for your life—how you would like for it to look. What kind of house would you like to live in? What would it look like? What color would it be? How many bedrooms would it have? I want you to get really visual on this.

I want you to decide exactly what kind of car you want to drive. I want you to decide how you want to dress. I want you to think about the area that you would like to live in, maybe the city you'd like to live in.

I'd like for you to picture the relationship that you'd like to have with your kids and maybe your parents and your spouse or your friendships. Picture those relationships in your mind.

Write those things down, and when you write them down, you will start to actually create that life for yourself. Take a few minutes right now, and create this new vision list.

Greater Expectations

The next way we sabotage our lives is through our expectations. We simply have very low expectations, and I believe people live either up to or down to exactly what you expect from them. We expect people to be late, to be rude, to do a half-assed job. Why? Because sadly, most people *are* late, they *are* rude, and they really *do* a half-assed job. We don't expect much from them, and they don't deliver much. When you experience bad service, are you surprised? No, because you probably didn't expect anything except bad service from the beginning. We get pretty much what we expect.

As employees, we don't expect much from our employers, and they don't prove us wrong very often. As employers, we sometimes don't expect much from our employees, and we don't get much more than that either.

Teenagers: we expect them to be rude, we expect them to be uninterested, and we expect them to be bored with everything that comes out of our mouths. They give us back exactly what we expect from them.

When you don't expect much from people, people simply won't deliver very much. What's the solution? Expect more from others. Are you just setting yourself up for disappointment? Absolutely. I promise you: when you expect a lot from others, they will disappoint you. On the other hand, sometimes—not often, but sometimes—they will surprise you. When that happens, stop and have a party. You see, I've decided it's better to be disappointed by expecting a lot from others and getting nothing than by expecting nothing from others and getting what I expected.

So I expect a lot from other people. I'd rather deal with a little bit of disappointment from time to time and still have high expectations. I actually expect people to deliver good service to me. I really do, and I've discovered that when my level of expectation goes up, their level of service goes up.

I expect the people who work for me to work very hard. How do I make sure that happens? I communicate my expectation in advance. I tell them what I expect from them. When you tell people what you expect from them, they have a higher chance of delivering it, because you have communicated your level of expectations.

I did that with my kids. I told them I expected them to give their very best. When they gave me their very best, I rewarded that. My kids did their best to give me their best because I communicated it clearly to them in advance.

It's easy to expect a lot from other people. All you really have to do is draw a kind of line in the sand and decide that you're not willing to compromise your standards. You then just have to communicate what those standards are to the people you're doing business with. You ask them for their word that they will do it, and you make them stand behind their word, or you don't do business with them.

That's pretty simple. It's just laying out expectations and communicating those expectations. It's easy to do with other people. Here's where it gets tough: you have to expect more from yourself. You have to draw a line in the sand for yourself. That's when you know how serious you are about personal development, about self-improvement, about turning your life around. When you're willing to draw that line in the sand in front of yourself and not compromise your own standards—even when no one's looking, even when no one else is going to find out, even where it would be a secret just between you and you—that's when you'll know how serious you really, really are. When you're willing to expect the best from yourself every single time, even when it's almost impossible, even when it's tough, even when it's humiliating, exhausting, you won't compromise your own personal standards. That's when you start to achieve things that very few people ever achieve.

It's easy to say, "I expect the best from myself," and then, when no one's looking, we don't really give the best. We can go away and tell them we gave our best.

I'm guilty of that sometimes myself. I'll go to the gym with my wife, and I'll say, "I'll meet you back here in thirty minutes." I'll get on the treadmill. I'm tired, and she doesn't understand I've been on a flight, I got in late, and all that. So she's doing a class or something, we'll meet up an hour later, and she'll say, "How was your thirty minutes on the treadmill?"

I'll go, "It was fine." I know there is no way in the world she would know that I didn't do thirty minutes on the treadmill, but *I* know I didn't. Whom did I cheat? Not her. She doesn't care. I cheated myself.

Often we cheat ourselves by compromising our own internal standards. Why? Because there's no way we can get caught, but you know what? We always get caught. We always get caught. We get caught by our substandard results. Results are everything. They can never be compromised. Results are everything.

That's how it really is. If you compromise along the way, you will receive substandard results. I don't want substandard results in my life, so I set very high expectations for myself and others, and I do my best to live up to my own expectations.

I created a family of high achievers. I have two sons. I always wanted my sons to give me their very best. I never expected them to be the best at whatever they undertook. I really didn't care if they were the best. I taught them not to care if they were the best. Instead I taught them to care completely about doing their best.

There's a huge difference. Sometimes you can try as hard as you want. You can do all the training in the whole world. You can practice day and night. You can do everything within your power, and you're still never going to be the best. You're just not. You don't have the talent for it. However, you can always give it your very best. That's all I ever ask from anyone. That's all I ever asked from my boys. That's what I taught them to expect from themselves—not to be the best, but to do their best. That's what I expect from myself. That's what they learned to expect from themselves.

My son, Patrick Winget, is a fashion designer. He and a buddy went into business when they were still in school at the Fashion Institute of Design and Merchandising in Los Angeles, and they struggled. They really had a hard time. They had lots of ideas;

they just didn't have any capital to finance them. However, they made it work. How? Hard work and a willingness to do whatever it took to succeed. That's really the key. They both lived on practically nothing. They worked nearly twenty hours a day, spent lots of nights sleeping on the floor of their cramped, trashy, little office manufacturing space stacked high with fabrics and patterns.

When Patrick did get a little money, he spent it on education, even though he was already going to school. He wouldn't even buy groceries. He'd buy fashion magazines in order to know about the next coming trend and be ahead of the curve. He told me just what I had said to him: you can always skip a meal, but you can't skip a chance for more education and inspiration. So he put his money into his future, knowing he'd be all right if he skipped lunch today, but he wouldn't be all right if he skipped an opportunity to learn more, to get a little more education, to stay ahead of the curve. He always wanted to stay on the edge so he would be ahead of everyone else.

In my opinion, no one was more willing to do what it took than these two guys. They worked hard. They did what it took to become successful, and eventually they made their little company work. They sold it and started another little company. Now they've gone their own ways, and Patrick is very successful, doing quite well, I will admit. I'm very proud of him, not because he became the best at running a little company or because he makes a lot of money. None of that was important as watching Patrick set a level of expectation for himself, draw a line in the sand, and say, "I gave my word. I have bills to pay. I have to commitments to make with my suppliers. I have commitments to make with the customers that bought from me. I'll do whatever it takes to make sure I keep my word, no matter what." That was his expectation of himself, and that's what he delivered, and that's what I'm most proud of about him.

My other son, Tyler, is a cop. He's a good cop. He was in the Army for eight years, and he was in the 82nd Airborne Division. He was in Iraq, and he was in Bosnia. When he came back, he wanted to be a cop. He'd always wanted to be a soldier or a cop. He's an adrenaline junkie. He craves excitement.

When he joined the Army, I went with him to meet with a recruiter. We weren't in a war at the time. They said, "Here are all your job opportunities: you could do this, and you could do that," and they mentioned all these different desk jobs.

"No," he said. "I want to carry a gun and blow things up." That was his goal. He wanted to be a real soldier who carried a gun and fought the bad guys. As a cop, he wants to carry a gun and fight bad guys. That's the kind of cop he is. He takes it very seriously. He likes the battles; he likes putting bad guys behind bars, and I admire that. In our society, we need people who are willing to do that job. I'm not willing to do it, but I'm glad somebody is, even if it's my son.

The key is that he expects himself to be the best version of a cop that he can possibly be. He spends his own money to take every training course that he can possibly attend, and he attends all kinds of courses at his own expense. He goes to the gym every single day so he'll be physically fit for any situation. He takes kickboxing and jujitsu and every other kind of hand-to-hand combat training because sometime, someday, he may just need that to save his own life or someone else's. He's willing to do whatever it takes in order to be the best, because that's what he expects from himself. I'm proud of him because of that.

I'm proud of myself because I taught them that as a father. That's the line in the sand I drew in my own life as a father: at least I would establish things I wanted to teach my boys, and it's all based on this one area where we sabotage our own lives.

We don't expect enough from ourselves. We expect ourselves to be the very best based on our own talents, based on our willingness to do whatever it takes. It's not whether you're the best; it's whether you've given the best, given the best of your abilities based on the talents that you have.

Have you done that? I'm betting you haven't. I still disappoint myself every single day because I know I could do more, and the way that I do more is by expecting more from myself.

What expectations do you have of yourself? Do you expect enough, or do you have low expectations based on your history, based on how you feel at the moment, based on the fact that you're tired, based on the fact that you say, "It never works out that well anyway, so what difference does it make?"

It doesn't matter what excuse you come up with. You have to create a new level of expectations for yourself. Here's what I want you to do. I want you to make a list of what you expect from yourself.

After you've made that list, I want you to go back and up the ante. I want you to expect more from yourself than you first wrote down, because I know that you can do more than you first thought. I know you can, and when you believe that you can, that's when you'll actually start to achieve more.

Facing the Consequences

The next way we sabotage ourselves is based on consequences. We need to understand that bad behavior creates consequences, and we have to feel the consequences of our bad behavior. We have to be willing to experience the pain of our mistakes, of our missteps, of our bad decisions. When we experience that pain, that's when we learn the lesson. There's no way to really learn the lesson in life unless you're willing to experience the pain yourself or let other people experience the pain.

I'm a big believer in consequences. I very much support feeling bad when you've done something wrong. I think that way too often we try to save people, and we don't end up saving them at all.

When I had my television show *Big Spender* on A&E, I pointed out how people had made huge, colossal mistakes with their finances, and they were in real trouble. When I pointed it out to them, I liked it when they cried. I wanted to see tears roll down their face. I wanted to see genuine remorse, because I believe when that we tie emotion to our stupidity, that's when we make real progress. Those people who say, "Oh, well, a lot of people get behind on their bills. It's not that big of a deal"—those people never fix their bills. It's when people go, "You're right. I haven't shown integrity. I feel bad about this. I've cheated my family. I haven't been fair to the creditors. I'm not serving myself well by doing this." They start to feel the pain. These are the people who really start to turn their lives around. We need to feel the pain of our consequences.

The most common question I get is, why do people do what they do? "Larry, why do people do the dumb things that they do? In 2017, 50 percent of Americans said they spend more money than they make. Why do they do that?" Why do people continue to do stupid things when they know the result is going to be horrific? Why do people smoke when they know they're going to die early? Why do people not exercise? Why do they eat too much? Why don't they spend more time with their families? Here's why. We all do what we do because we're allowed to do it. That's simply what it comes down to. We can get by with it. Remember the old joke: why does a dog lick himself? Because he can. Why do people do what they do? Because they can. No one's there to stop them.

The only thing that keeps us in check is consequences. Consequences control our behavior. If we don't allow people to experience the consequences of their behavior, we've cheated them. If your kid throws a ball in the living room and breaks a lamp and you don't do anything about it, chances are, next time he's going to throw that ball in the living room again. The only way you're going to teach him that that is unacceptable behavior is to impose some painful consequences on him.

The same thing is true in how we run our businesses. If you give me bad service, and I'm willing to continue to pay for it and never point out the fact that you're giving me bad service, I can pretty much assure myself of bad service during my whole relationship with you. But when I point out that I'm not willing to accept that bad service, and I impose the consequences of giving me bad service by complaining, by writing a letter, by telling other people, by stopping spending my money with you, you will feel the pain of your bad behavior, because I will impose it on you.

Sometimes you have to impose your own pain. Sometimes you have to impose the consequences for your bad behavior upon yourself, because you're the only one who knows about it.

What kind of pain am I talking about? Maybe you need to experience a little remorse. Remorse can be painful. I'm a big believer in remorse—feeling bad, feeling terrible about something you've done that's stupid, feeling disappointment in yourself because you didn't give it your very best. I'm about the only guy I know in this business that talks about remorse. I think it's because we want a happier way. We say, "Oh, don't feel bad." Well, maybe you ought to feel bad. "Oh, it's OK." Maybe it's not OK. "Oh, don't worry about it." Why not? Maybe you should worry about it: you've been stupid. Feeling bad when you've made a mistake, when you've done something stupid, is a way of feeling a little pain from your consequences so you won't be as prone to repeat that bad behavior again.

You see, there's always, always, always some kind of consequence. We have to experience consequences. If we didn't, we would have utter chaos. In fact, the whole reason that we have limits and contracts and codes and laws and rules, even fences, is to establish ethical, moral, and physical boundaries for society to live by. If we didn't, we would have chaos. Because we have those things, we live in a fairly peaceful, reasonable manner.

Games have rules. Life has rules. If you break the rules, you experience the consequences. Can you imagine a game of checkers with no rules? We'd have people just screaming, "King me, king me," just because they showed up. Even in hockey, you can have a fistfight, knock out a guy's teeth, and still keep playing the game. It has a consequence, though, and that consequence is called a penalty box. That's the special little place you go to when you break too many of the rules or break them too severely.

Life has a penalty box too. We don't call it that, because we don't consider our results to be penalties, but they are. In life, the penalty box is called sickness. It's called unemployment, poverty, unhappiness, maybe even loneliness. You probably never thought about those things as penalties before, but they are. Each of those situations is a penalty. It is a consequence for the way you've been living your life. It's a consequence based on your decisions, your ideas, your belief, your thoughts, your words, and your actions. Most people, sadly, don't seem to be able to correlate their behavior with the results. Instead, they either call it bad luck or just want to blame someone else, like society.

We all experience the consequences of our choices. Painful they may be, but those consequences are our lessons. If we ignore the lessons, we will be doomed to repeat them. So when are feeling the pain of your consequences, welcome it. I know that sounds ridiculous, but that pain will teach you that you don't want to do that behavior again. Why? It hurts too much. So feel the pain of your consequences; learn from your consequences so you can stop that behavior and start to do the right thing instead.

Here's what I want you to do next. I want you to make a list of all the things that have gone wrong in your life, all the pain that you're currently experiencing, and realize that that pain is a consequence of something that you've done wrong. I want you to track backwards from the pain to the action to the thought to the words to the beliefs that created the consequence that created the pain. When you do that, and you start to follow that logic, it will help you determine in the future what action you ought to take, what you ought to say, what you ought to do differently so you don't have to experience that pain again.

I promise you this is a very beneficial exercise to go through. It will take a little time, and it will be painful along the way, but I promise you that the pain of doing this will be well worth the reward.

Sabotage and Habits

The next way we sabotage our life is through our bad habits. It's really very simple. Habits are created by doing things the same way over and over again.

Say that the first time you ever put on your socks, you put the sock on your left foot first. The next day, you put on your sock on your left foot first again, and you did it that way again the third time.

Before you knew it, that became your habit. Your left sock went on first. If you tried to put your right sock on first, it would feel foreign and weird to you. Why? Because you'd be breaking a habit that was established a long time ago.

We don't even realize things are habits until it's too late or too weird and painful to change them. That's not a big deal when it comes to putting on your socks. Who cares whether you start with your right foot or your left foot? It does become a big deal when those habits are detrimental to your success, your future, your family, your health, your finances. Those habits are just as painful and difficult to break as it would be if I told you to start with a different foot when you put on your socks tomorrow.

Those habits can ruin your life. The key is to recognize them early so you can get control of them. You need to recolonize your bad habits.

Sometimes when I mention bad habits to people, they'll say, "But, Larry, I don't smoke, I don't drink, and I don't really eat too much, so I don't really have any bad habits."

You know I'm not letting you off that easily. Bad habits are a lot more than the negative things that get so well publicized. Bad habits are, usually and sadly, the habits that are most subtle and most damaging—so subtle we sometimes don't even recognize them as such.

I have a few friends who are habitually late. They don't think there's anything wrong with telling me they'll meet me at a restaurant at 7:00 and showing up at 7:20. It doesn't hit them that being twenty minutes for an agreed-to time is unacceptable. They don't understand that they have been disrespectful of my time. They don't understand that when we had a 7:00 reservation at the restaurant, the restaurant counted on us being there at 7:00 and that it was disrespectful to the restaurant and disrespectful to the diners who had that same table reserved for 8:30. They don't get that. They don't understand that's a bad habit.

We can carry this idea over to dealing with customers. You can lose customers by disrespecting their time in showing up ten minutes late. You say, "Hey, it's only ten minutes." No, it's late, and it's more than late, it's disrespectful. It's more than disrespectful, it's a lack of integrity. It's more than a lack of integrity—you lied. "Larry, it can't be that. I didn't lie. I was just late." No, you said you would be there, and you didn't show up. That one little bad habit of being late tells me you're a liar and you're disrespectful of my time. As a customer, I won't allow you to do that to me. You don't get to be my friend for very long either. That's how it works. That's the line that I've drawn in the sand. That's what I expect from people. All these things tie together.

Bad grammar is a bad habit. So is dressing like a slob or not being able to communicate your thoughts effectively. These things can ruin your chances for success. Lots of little things that you may not even understand have become habits can absolutely ruin your chances for becoming successful.

I talked to a person who said that one reason she was having a hard time with her finances was that she always met her friends on Saturday morning. They would go out for a big breakfast and coffee. Then they would go to the mall and shop and have a nice lunch and a glass of wine. Then, they would go home, and that's how they spent every Saturday. She said, "How can I be expected to save money when that's been my habit for the last several years with my friends?"

I said, "How is that habit affecting your finances?"

"But, Larry, it's what I do on Saturdays."

"Well," I said, "I suggest you find something else to do on Saturdays. You have to break that habit."

She didn't want to do that. She wasn't willing to break that habit. In other words, she wasn't willing to take control of her life. It wasn't important to her. She didn't give a damn about her financial security.

She gave more of a damn about spending Saturday with her friends, because that had become her habit.

All of these things tie together. We end up sabotaging our finances and ruining our chances at success simply because we're not willing to recognize that it hurts when we do it. Until you're willing to say, "It hurts when I do this"—admitting that you have some bad habits that are sabotaging your success—you're not going to get any better.

So you need some new habits. You need habits that move you closer to where you want to be instead of farther from where you want to be. Everything in life either moves you closer to where you want to be or moves you farther away. Remember I said life is black or white. There's no gray. Every action you take, every thought you have, every word you say, everything you do, think, and believe either moves you closer to your goals or moves you farther away from your goals. If you do certain things, think those things, say those things long enough, they will become habits that can sabotage your success.

You have to recognize these habits and create some new ones. Let me tell you about creating new habits. You can't just say, "I'm going to do things differently." How are you going to do that? How do you create the habit of eating more healthily? You don't break the habit of eating unhealthy foods until you create the habit of eating healthy foods, which means you have to go to the store and buy healthy foods and stock your pantry and your refrigerator with healthy food. You have to replace the bad habit of buying the wrong things with the habit of buying the healthy things. You can't stop a bad habit until you start a new habit.

How do you stop watching television? Do you just sit on the couch, turn the TV off, and say, "Now I'm not watching television"? That really wasn't the goal, was it? The goal was not to sit there but to become more active in your life, so you can't just stop watching television and start saying that you're going to become active. Instead you have to have a new habit, a new behavior, a new action to replace the old, bad habit, which means you have to have a plan. You have to have exercise that you're willing to do. You have to have a game laid out on a table that you can play with your family. You have to have walking shoes so you can take that walk down the street. You have to have a new habit to replace the old habit.

Don't just say, "I have the willpower to stop." Willpower is a joke. Willpower is overrated. Let's say your habit is to eat a big dinner, sit around on your butt watching TV for three or four hours until you drop off to sleep, wander into the bedroom, and crash until the alarm goes off the next morning. Then you have to get up and go to work. By the way, I've just described the typical evening of about 80 percent of all adults in our country today.

If that's your habit, chances are, you're overweight and you're lazy, which is the result of doing that night after night. If that is your result, you just might want to break that habit. How are you going to do it? You have the willpower just to stop? No, you don't just stop doing that. Willpower alone won't change it. What's going to change it is having something new ready to take the place of that behavior. You're going to have to get up from the dinner table immediately, clean it off, wash the dishes, and put the food away, and you're going to have to have an activity planned. You can't count on willpower to keep you from sitting down in front of the television. You have to have an activity to replace it with.

Here's what I want you to do. Just figure out your habits. Figure out what you're doing over and over every day, and then give yourself some new habits. Write down a list of things that you could replace the bad habits with. You have to have the replacement list, because you don't have the willpower to just stop doing the wrong thing. You have to have some right things lined up.

"How do I know what I should quit doing, Larry?" If it's not moving you closer to your goal, then you ought to quit doing it. "How do I know whether that will work?" The only way is to try, but you're smart enough to look at what you've been doing and to know whether or not it is moving you closer to your goals of being healthier, more successful, and financially secure. You know in your gut whether the things that you're doing move you closer to your goals or farther away from them. If they're moving you closer, keep doing them. If they're moving you farther away, stop and do something else.

My goal for you right now is to write down what you've been doing wrong and what you could replace those things with. Take a moment now to make those lists.

Role Models

Here's the next way that we sabotage our lives. It comes down to our role models. You're saying, "Larry, I don't really have any role models," or "I can't see where that applies."

We all have role models. Let me give you some examples. I grew up on a farm. I like everything that has fur and everything that has feathers. On the farm I grew up on, we had a lot of different chickens and geese, and I saw that geese would imprint. You've seen that on television.

In fact, there was a great movie years ago called *Fly Away Home.* These geese were born, and because the mother had been killed, the first thing they saw was people. They never learned how to fly, because their role model was people. They didn't have an example of how to fly, so these people had to teach these geese how to fly, and they used a plane. It was a great movie.

That's how it really works. I've been around geese, and I see that they do imprint. If you become their role model, they will become more like you, and they will follow you around all the time. That's exactly how all of us are as people. We imprint on the things that we see the most in our lives.

When you're growing up at your family table, you watch how your parents eat, how they hold their fork, how they hold their knife, how they put their spoon in their soup. Whether they have good table manners or bad, that's what you learn. That becomes your role model, and you repeat that behavior until it becomes your habit.

The same thing applies with your grammar, how you speak, and the accent that you have. It's what we were imprinted with from the time of our birth. We all imprint on the things that we observed growing up.

When I was growing up, my dad didn't like football. We never watched any football on TV. All I ever heard him say was, "I don't really like football." What's amazing is, I don't like football either. Why? Nothing against the game of football. It's just that I was never given as an example from living with my dad that football was a good game to watch. My dad liked boxing. We always watched the Friday night fights. Because my dad always liked boxing and watched the Friday night fights, and I sat there with him and we ate a big bowl of popcorn together, I grew up liking boxing, not football. In fact, right now I can see that there's going to be a boxing match on television, and I start getting hungry for popcorn, because I was imprinted: boxing, popcorn, sitting on the couch.

We all learn that way. We learn by watching other people: parents, older brothers and sisters, aunts and uncles and teachers, and people we watch on television. We all learn to act in a certain way from watching the people we are exposed to.

Your parents taught you what was acceptable and what was unacceptable behavior on the basis of their actions. They became your example, and you followed it until your own experiences, your knowledge base, and your circle of influence expanded. Then you learned new ways of acting based on what you were shown.

As a parent, you set the example for your own children as well. So what kind of example are you setting? The example you're setting is the example your kids will learn. If you have behaviors you don't want your kids to model, then you need to change those behaviors now.

I really do believe life is pretty simple. You have to take responsibility for your actions. You have to learn from consequences. You have to get the education that's necessary, and you can do that by reading. It doesn't have to be complicated.

My philosophy is: make a decision, make the right decision. If it sounds like a good idea, try it. Even if you make the wrong decision, you'll find out. Stay active, do something to take control of our life. It's about self-help. You have to help yourself.

One of the most important quotes that I've heard recently says, "The best helping hand you will ever find is at the end of your own wrist." Know that you can help yourself out of any situation by taking responsibility for it and taking control of it. Don't deny the situation. Get the education you need to fix it, and then take action.

You can even be your own role model. Look at the successes you've had in the past. Remind yourself that you're not a loser. Sometimes you win: build on those wins; build on those successes. Build on those victories to remind yourself that you have the ability to get past challenges.

Realize that your behavior is pretty much learned behavior based on observing other people. Realize that you can observe different people who would be better role models for you, and that you can become your own role model.

Take a moment right now to create a list of the role models you've had in your life. Determine whether they've taught you things that really were able to help you be more successful. Determine whether they taught you things that were valuable. Then look at your own life and realize that you can learn from yourself using your own victories and successes.

The Missing Plan

Here's the last and perhaps the most important way we end up sabotaging our lives: we don't have a plan. It's amazing how few people actually have written down a plan for their lives. Notice I said "*written down* a plan." Everybody has a plan: "I wish this would happen." How's that wishing working out for you?

Hope is not a strategy for success. Wishful thinking is not a strategy for success. A plan is a strategy for success. For as long as I've been in the personal development industry—and that's been a good long while now—I've heard a statistic. It's backed up by many different sources. The statistic says that only 3 percent of our society have written down plans for their lives; the other 97 percent don't. Amazingly, the 3 percent who have written plans do better in every area than the other 97 percent put together. Wouldn't you want to be one of the 3 percent? Why aren't you? Is it because you're lazy? Is it because you didn't know any better?

No more excuses now. You have to have a plan. You need to have a written plan. See why I've been big on making these lists? It's about writing things down. It's about working with a document.

Here's the way it works with a plan. Let's say you had a vacation coming up. You'd have a plan for that vacation. You'd know where you wanted to go and what you wanted to do along the way. You would know how you planned on getting there. You would know whom you wanted to go with, and you would have a good idea of what it was going to cost for you to take this vacation.

Those are the five elements of planning your vacation. Those five elements also go into planning your day off. You'd know where you were going, what you were going to do when you got there, how you were going to get there, how much it was going to cost, and whom you were going with. That just makes sense.

Do you know those five things about the rest of your life? Chances are, you don't. You don't have a written plan for where you would like to end up in all areas of your life, do you? If you do, you're one of the 3 percent.

Most people don't. They don't know where they want to end up. They don't know what they want to do along the way. They don't have a list of things: "I'm going to make sure I don't miss this. I have to make sure I take advantage of that. I have to make sure this happens." They don't have a list of how they're going to make it happen. They've never written down exactly how much it's going to cost. Most people don't even know whom they want with them on this journey. They don't have a plan for their lives.

You have to get a plan. The good thing is that this is really one of the simplest things to fix. This is the probably easiest of all methods of fixing your life and getting out of your own way.

The first thing it takes is paper. Get out a big, old stack of paper. Start to write down everything that you would like to have happen. Make it a big list. Dream big when you're writing these things down. Don't have any small ideas. Don't have any small plans. Write down what you'd really like for your life to look like, and you have to have a variety of lists. You have a variety of areas in your life, so you need a different list for every area.

What do you want your life to look like financially? How do you want to be physically in terms of your health, your appearance, how much you weigh, how fit you are? What do you want your marriage, your relationships with your kids and your parents and your friends to look like?

How do you want to be mentally? How smart do you want to be? How many books are you willing to read? How many lectures are you willing to go to? What are you going to do socially? How are you going to do more in your career? How about spiritually? In fact, I even think you need a list of secret stuff, things that you plan to work on for your own self-satisfaction. You don't need to share it with anybody else. This is *your* list.

Once you have all these areas defined and you've started working on this list, realize this is not the end-all, be-all list. You can go back to it every day if you want—several times a day—and add things and take things off as they become less important to you. This is where you establish the priorities for every area of your life, and you put together a plan. Remember those questions: Where do I want to end up? What do I want to do along the way? What do I want to make sure I don't miss along the way? How do I plan on getting there? How much is it going to cost me? Have a budget for your plan. And whom do I want to involve in achieving my plan?

This is an important issue, but most people never take the time to make a plan. That's what I want you to do. Get some paper. Get out a pen. How simple is that? Start to write things down. Once you have a written plan for your life, that's when you start to become more successful. I'm not a big believer in magic, but this is like creating magic in your life.

The Magic of Giving Up

Everybody wants to get more success. We all want to get more money. We all want to get more healthy. We all want to get more out of our relationships. Let me tell you this: you don't get more of anything ever. You're not going to get more successful, more financially secure. You don't *get* more. You become more by giving up more.

Yup, that's what it comes down to. You have to give up the things that are keeping you from being successful. I think we're all basically wired for success, but we let a lot of things get in the way. We're too busy about things that don't matter: the mundane, the superficial, the things that don't count. We have to be willing to give those things up in order to leave ourselves room for success.

How do you get healthier? By giving up the things that are keeping you from being healthy. How do you get more financially secure? By giving up the things that are keeping you from being financially secure. How do you get a better relationship with your spouse? By giving up the things that are keeping you from having a great relationship with your spouse. How do you get better at your job? By giving up the things that keep you from being better at your job.

See how it works? What are you willing to give up? If you're not willing to adjust your lifestyle and give things up, you're never going to achieve success. Everything that I've talked about comes down to a willingness to do what it takes, to give up what stands between you and what you want.

So, understanding that you're going to have to give some things up along the way, you need to make a list. You need to be willing to sit down right now with one of those sheets of paper and write

down some things that you're willing to give up—
the things that are standing between where you are
and where you want to be. If you don't put anything
on this list, you can't move forward. Take a few
moments now to work on that list, your give-up list.

Three Steps for Fixing Your Life

So here's where we are. I've given you all the different ways that you sabotage your life, and now you're
saying, "OK, OK, I get it. Now what do I do?"

You need to do three things to fix your life:
First, recognize where you are. Recognition is the
first step. Recognition is key. Recognize the situation that you're in. Recognize that you need to fix it.
Recognize that you've made mistakes. Recognize too
that you've done well in some areas. Know where
you are, know where you'd like to be, know what's
keeping you from where you'd like to be. Know what
you're willing to give up in order to achieve what
you want. That is the recognition step.

Next, education. You have to have the information it takes to move from where you are to the
place that you really want to be. This means you
have to read, you have to ask people questions. The
more information you arm yourself with, the better
off you will be in moving forward and being able to

handle any situation. Education is key. Fortunately, we've removed part of that obstacle for you, because you've already gotten a little education about what you can do, but there's always more information out there. There's always more that you can learn about, whatever situation you're in.

Number one is recognition, and number two is education. Number three is application. Some of you are saying, "Of course, just apply what I've learned, Larry. Of course, duh." That's not how it is. *Application* is not that fancy a word, but it's a fancier word for the ugliest, nastiest, most vulgar, four-letter word in our society. That word is *work*.

Yup, that's the ugliest word in our whole vocabulary: work. And that's what application means: work. You have to go to work on this stuff. People would rather do anything than work. They'd rather have success be attracted to them. I know that's popular, but I don't think that's the way success really works. I've tried for years to sit back, be lazy, and hope that would I attract success. It never did. I had to work for success.

It always comes down to work. That's why most people never achieve what they want in life: they're not willing to work. You have to break a sweat. People go, "I thought it was going to be easy." No. It's not easy. Success is hard. It's not complicated, but it's still hard, because it requires work. You have to be willing to go to work.

You're finally to the point where you say, "OK, Larry, I get it. I have to go to work. I'll go to work. What should I do first?"

You see, that's the magic part. In fact, this plan is so easy that you're going to be amazed. What should you do? Here's my answer: do anything. Yeah, that's right. Just do anything. Do anything different than you have in the past, and you will get a different result. That's the way action works. You do anything different, you will get a different result.

Here's an idea. You're used to brushing your teeth with your right hand. Why don't you brush your teeth with your left hand? "Larry, will that work?" I don't know; it can't hurt.

You sleep on the right side of the bed. Why don't you sleep on the left side? "Larry, that doesn't even make sense. Will that work?" I don't know. It might make you so uncomfortable that you get up a little earlier. As long as you're up, why don't you exercise? Why don't you go for a walk? Why don't you read a book? Why don't you do something while you're up? You're not sleeping anyway.

It doesn't matter *what* you do; it matters *that* you do. You have to do something differently. Here's the cool part about it: If you do just a little bit differently, you'll get just a little bit better results. If you do a whole lot, chances are you'll get a whole lot better results. But here again, it's one of those magical things. Sometimes you can do a little bit and you'll get a lot better results. I don't know how that works. Sometimes one, small action can create an amazing result. Which is the action that will create the magic result? I don't know. The key is to get busy. You have to do a lot of things.

Will everything you do work? No, it won't. Probably only about half of what you do will work. The key is to do a lot of stuff. If what you've been doing in the past hasn't been working for you, I suggest you do a lot of stuff differently in the future. When you start seeing a good result from one action, repeat that action. If you don't see a good result from that action, then dump it. Pretty soon you'll have weeded through all of your actions, and you'll have a list of actions that work. You'll know what it's going to take for you to move farther ahead. See how simple this really is?

Don't ever think anything that comes out of Larry Winget's mouth is going to be based on thinking your way to success. It doesn't work that way. With me, it's about taking action and working your way to success. I'm not going to kid you. Success comes from hard work.

Today, Not Tomorrow

I've given you some good ideas. I haven't lied to you. I told you it was going to be a lot of hard work, and it will be. The key is right now you have some ideas. You have some ideas of what you could do differently in order to create new results. I know you want new results. That's why you bought this book. So if you've gotten one good idea, when would be the time to actually start on that good idea? The answer is now. If you're going to write something down that will really help you every single day, I want you to write down these three letters, TNT. TNT. It stands for *today, not tomorrow*. When would it be good to start on a plan that will help you turn your life around so you'll be more financially secure, more successful, have better relationships, have more money, be healthier? Right now. Don't wait until tomorrow.

Here's my goal for you. Find one actionable idea that you can start on today, because taking action today will help you create the future that you've always wanted.

Now you understand the importance of taking action, and taking action right now. How do you take action and start to really make a change in your life? Let me give you eight fast steps that will help you.

1. Decide to change. Just make the decision to change. The decision that you're not going to live the way you have in the past and will do things differently is going to be powerful in your life.

2. Know why it is important for you to change. There has to be a reason. *How* you're going to do it is not nearly as important as *why* it's necessary for you to do it.

3. Be willing to do whatever it takes. That willingness to do whatever it takes will set you apart from the rest of the pack.

4. Actually do whatever it takes to change. You have to apply action to your willingness. Prove that you're willing by taking the action.

5. Realize that you're going to make some mistakes along the way. You're going to fail. You're going to be disappointed. When you fail, shake it off, and just start again. Big deal—you messed up. Get started again.

6. Once you get there, when you've arrived and you've accomplished your goal, have a cele-

bration. That's right: it's OK to stop and have a celebration. This is not all about the work. This is sometimes about the enjoyment. You accomplished something. Be happy for yourself. Have a celebration.

7. Move on. The best time to start on your next idea is when you're on the heels of a victory, when you feel the power and the confidence that comes through success. Use that success, that momentum, to move on to the next idea.

8. Become totally committed to your own success. Become totally committed to being the best version of you that you can possibly be. Be totally committed to doing whatever it takes so you can repeat this process over and over again.

When you do these eight steps, you can achieve the life that you've always dreamed up and actually have it happen. You can take the lists that you've been working on and you can say, "How do these eight steps apply?"

First of all, when you look at these lists of what you're going to do differently in your life, decide whether they're really important for you. Are they important enough for you to really be willing to do whatever it takes? Do you understand that as you look at some of these things on your list, they are going to be challenging and that you will fail along the way?

You have to understand that that's OK. The thing on these lists are going to be hard. They are going to be very challenging for you, and you will experience some disappointment and failure along the way.

I'm telling you: big deal. Shake it off. Keep going. Keep going through your list. Always be moving forward. It's about building momentum. That's the reality of success—little, bitty steps along the way.

It's not going to be an overnight change. You didn't create the mess that you're living right now overnight; you're not going to fix it overnight. This is a process, and the process will work for you because of the eighth step. It's your commitment to the process. It's your commitment to being the best version of you that you could possibly be. It's your commitment to knowing you can do this if you're willing to work hard enough. I know you can. Now just get out there and do it. When you've done it, don't forget: stop, enjoy yourself, and have a celebration. In the next chapter I'll be covering some more solutions and giving you even more fixes.

3
How to
Get Things Done

You can probably tell by now that I'm a big believer in making lists. I like lists for everything that's gone wrong with your life and for everything you want to accomplish in life. You need a document that you can refer to. First of all, when you write it down, it allows you to focus. You can actually see in black-and-white, right in front of you, exactly what you're dealing with, whether it be positive or negative, whether it be looking back at your past to know exactly what you've done wrong, or looking toward the future to know what could happen if you're willing to work hard enough.

So in this chapter, there will be a lot of list making. As we go through these lists, you're going to find lots of different areas where you could start to make some real changes.

Taking Responsibility

It starts with my number-one principle for turning your life around. This can't come as a surprise to you. I've been talking about it throughout this book. It's the reason I'm called the pit bull of personal development, because it's the one thing I get my teeth into and never let go of. That thing is taking responsibility.

When it comes to getting out of your own way, nothing helps more than taking responsibility. You need to sit down and make a list about taking responsibility. Now you're saying, "That doesn't even make sense, Larry. How do you make a list about taking responsibility?"

Here's what I want you to do. Get a sheet of paper, get a pen, and write down at the top "Taking Responsibility." Then write down everything you can think of that you feel is keeping you from being successful, in every area of your life.

What's keeping you from being successful at work? Do you know? Some things come to mind immediately; I know they do. What's keeping you from having as much money as you would like or from having great relationships with your significant other, your kids, your family, your parents? What's keeping you from driving the kind of car you'd like to drive or from living in the house you've always dreamed of or from dressing the way you'd like to dress? Name everything in the world that comes to mind that's keeping you from having exactly what you want.

Put down why you're broke. Put down why you're not as healthy as you'd like to be. Put down why you weigh more than you'd like to weigh. Write it all down. I want this to be a list where you whine and complain and put down everything that makes you mad about your life. Write it all down. Don't skip this. This is important.

When you get to the end of the list, here's what I want you to do: I want you to draw a big X through it, and write down your name, because *you* are the only thing on that list that matters. *You* are the reason you're not doing well at work. *You* are the reason your relationships aren't the way you want them to be. *You* are the reason you weigh what you weigh.

I really do contend that your life is exactly the way you want it to be; otherwise it would be different. Don't argue with me about this. You're not going to win. Your thoughts, your words, your choices, your actions, your decisions created the life that you have, and you are the one that has to get out of your way in order to turn your life around. All of that starts with taking responsibility for the way your life is.

Once you've done that, I want you to go to the mirror. I want you to look yourself in the eye. Then I want you to say these words. This is an affirmation that I wrote. You can rewrite this any way you want to, but you need to have a talk with yourself. This is what I suggest:

Look yourself in the eye and say, *"My thoughts, my words, and my actions have created the life I am living. I take complete responsibility for everything going on in my life. I will stop blaming others. I will never again offer any excuses to myself or anyone else. I am in charge of my life and my results from this moment on, and I am taking control now."*

If you like it, use this version. If you want to do your own version that sounds more as if it came out of your mouth, do that. Then I want you to repeat that every single day. Yes, repeat it daily, because you need to hear from your own lips every single day that you're responsible for your life and that you are in control of your life .

This is called an *affirmation*. Normally I'm not a big believer in affirmations, because affirmation without implementation is nothing but self-delusion. If you think you can only say these words and have your life turn around, you're crazy. You have to do more than say the words.

I've been constantly saying that you have to work, work, work. That's what it always comes down to. You have to be able to work on what you say. Now that you've said these words, you have to actually go out and work to make this happen. You can't say the words alone. You have to put action to your words.

How do you do that? You keep your word. In fact, it's all based on my number-one rule for both life and business: *do what you said you would do, when you said you would do it, the way you said you would do it.* If you don't do those things, you're a liar. You don't want to be known as a liar, not to yourself or anybody else, so when you tell somebody you're going to do something, you do it. When do you do it? When you said you would do it. How do you do it? Exactly the way you said you would do it.

If you run your business that way, that's all your customers are ever going expect or want from you. They want you to do what you said you would do, when you said you would do it, the way you said you would do it.

That's what your family wants from you. That's what your spouse, your kids want from you—and by the way, that's exactly what you want from them. That's what your boss wants from you. That's what you want from your employees. We all want the people we deal with personally and professionally to do exactly what they said they would do, when they said they would do it, the way they said they would do it. This philosophy of life is based on personal responsibility. Practice it, and everyone you deal with on every level will respect you more. Every time you're tempted to slack off or do or be a little less than you could, remember that you are a person of integrity who lives by the simple creed: *do what you said you would do, when you said you would do it, the way you said you would do it.*

It's about the *Why*

What should you do? You need to go back to the list. You need to write down why this is important to you. Again, notice what I just said: *why* this is important to you. I'm not nearly as focused on *how* you're going to do these things as I am on why. If you ask a guy how to get rich, there are as many ways to get rich as there are rich people. If you want to know how to do something, go to Google and type in, "How do I . . . ?" and put in anything in the whole world. You'll get hundreds of answers on how you should do something.

How is fine. There are lots of ways to do things, but *why* is what's really important. Why do I need to do this? Why do I need to make this change? Why do I need to take responsibility for my life?

Only you can answer that. No one can answer that for you except you. Why do I need to do it? If your *why* is strong enough, you can endure any *how*. You can get bogged down in the *how*. Once you're in the middle of it, you can get disappointed and frustrated, and you'll come up against a brick wall sometimes. Sometimes you'll be tempted to quit, but the motivation comes from a really strong *why*. The reason you're doing this—that's what will keep you going in the face of anything.

So right now, take a pen, put it to paper, and determine why it is important, maybe for the very first time in your life, for you to take responsibility and for you to take control of your life.

As we go through all of these ideas, I'm going to be asking you, "Why do you want to do this?" If you can't come up with why it's important, then don't bother, because it's the *why* that will keep you on track and will keep you motivated and moving forward.

Accomplishment, Not Activity

You want to get more done? Of course you do; everybody does. I always hear the excuse, "But I'm busy. Larry, you don't understand what I have going on. I have a lot on my plate. How could I possibly get more done? I'm so busy right now, I can't even think." I'm busy too, and still I'm always trying to figure out ways to get more done. If you'd like to get more done, let me give you some ideas.

First of all, focus on accomplishment, not on activity. Too many people are focused on whether they're doing things. Who cares? It doesn't matter what you're doing if you're not doing the thing that moves you farther along toward your goal, closer to where you really want to be. Remember, it's not what you do that really matters; it's what you get done.

In fact, if you have any to-do lists (and we all love our little to-do lists), throw those away. You don't need any to-do lists. There's plenty to do without putting it on a list. Instead, have a *to-get-done* list. To get done means I've accomplished something. It's behind me now. I did it. It's over. I won. I'm victorious.

See what I mean? It changes your whole mind-set from *to-do* to *to-get-done*. You need to focus on the accomplishment of the task, not working on the task. That will allow you to get more done. Just think about accomplishment.

Next, I want you to have a written plan. Surprise, surprise—you have to write something down. You have to have a plan every single day for what you want, not to do, but to get done. Work from document. All the time remind yourself of those words: *work from document.* Have a sheet of paper that you can keep with you, in front of you, in your pocket, that says, "This is what has to get done today." It doesn't matter what you do. This is what has to get done today.

Then I want you to refuse to become involved in things that get in the way. I know that's challenging, but you have to learn to say no to some things. You can't be one of those people who says, "Sure, I'll help you. Yeah, OK, I'll do that." At some point, you have to realize that what you need to get done is so important that you can't lose focus, so you have to get good at saying no to some things. It's OK to say no. People aren't used to that, and they may think you're rude, but all you have to do is say, "No, I can't help you. No, I'm not going to do that. No, I don't want to do that." Why? Because this is what has to get done today, and I can't do anything else until this gets done.

This is a problem especially in business, where most of us get caught up in going to meetings. Meetings are one of the biggest time killers in business today. You can't argue with that. You've been to a lot of meetings where you just sit around and talk, and nothing gets done. Here's my rule for having a meeting: if it doesn't have an agenda, you don't need to have it.

Here's a great idea for meetings: stand up. Meetings don't last nearly as long when people are standing. The problem is, we come in, we make sure everybody sits down. They have their coffee, and they have some snacks in front of them. We make sure everybody has a sheet of paper in front of them and a pad and pencils and all that stuff. Is everybody comfortable? Is the room all right? How's the temperature? We spend so much time getting comfortable that we don't want to leave the meeting.

Instead, make your meetings uncomfortable. When you walk into the room and say, "We need to have a meeting," tell everybody to pull the chairs out of the conference room and stand up. The meeting won't last nearly as long. When you've accomplished what it set out to do, stop. Say, "OK, it's done," and turn around and walk out.

I'm a big believer in having meetings when they're necessary and when something needs to get done, but I don't think they need to go on for very long, so don't let a meeting ruin your entire day.

Here's another idea for getting more things done, and this works in business or in your personal life: complete one thing before you start the next. I know there's a lot of talk about multitasking, and that's terrific if you can actually do it, but it's hard for some people to have four or five things going on at the same time. So figure out what the most important thing is, the thing that has to get done—not the thing that would be nice to get done, but the thing that you absolutely must get done. When you figure that out, make sure it gets done. Then you can move to the next task and the next one and the next, but make sure the most important one gets done first.

You also need to watch out for the telephone and for emails. You have to watch out for text messages and social networking sites. They are addictive, and if you're not careful, they can overrun your life until you're not getting anything done. Yeah, you're busy, but you're not busy doing the right things. So be aware of all those little distractions that come up.

Here's a great idea if you're at work: shut the door to your office. Now you may be saying, "Larry,

I don't have a door. I work in a cubicle." That's OK; here's a great idea for you. Next time you're staying in a hotel room, you know the little "Do not disturb "sign that you hang on your door so the maid won't bother you early the next morning? Take that sign. Yes, I'm advocating that you steal the sign. They've got more, trust me.

Take that sign. If you have a cubicle, put a thumb-tack in the sign or tape it up right at the opening to your cubicle. If you have a door, hang it on the doorknob. Realize that there comes a time in getting things done where you need some peace and quiet and solitude so you can focus. There's nothing rude about saying that the work is more important than the conversation. In fact that's what you're paid for. You're paid for the work.

A long time ago, we talked about the importance of having an open-door policy, and managers loved to say, "I have a totally open-door policy. People can come in anytime they need to talk to me."

I'm sorry: that's stupid. An open-door policy is not a good idea. People will wander in and bother you, and they'll get you involved in meaningless chatter that doesn't need to happen and doesn't move anyone any closer to getting the work done. It's OK to shut your door.

Here's another idea for work: if you want to get more done, do it when not many people are around. This means during breaks and lunch hours and before others come in and after they go home. Have you noticed that people are a distraction? So if you have something important to do, avoid them.

Let's make it even more personal. You want to get more done at home? Here's a great idea. It goes back to what I said about meetings. Stand up more. You don't get very much done when you're just sitting around. I've noticed that, haven't you? When you're just sitting around, you don't get much done.

You're saying, "Larry, when I get home, all I want to do is sit around." Yet you'll complain tomorrow that you didn't get the laundry done, or you didn't get the house dusted, or you didn't vacuum, or you didn't make dinner. That's because you were sitting around. Why don't you stand up? It's a very simple suggestion. You're probably laughing at my idea, but you need to trust me on this one. Stand up. Wander through your house. I do this a lot. In fact, I'm sort of a stander anyway; I like to stand up and wander around my house. As you do, you'll notice things that need to be done. You'll see a pillow that's out of alignment or a magazine that needs to be picked up or a newspaper from yesterday that's lying there all spread out, or you'll notice that your kid left an empty glass on the coffee table. You'll become aware of things that need to be done around the house. When you see them, don't put them off. Do them right now.

You find those things when you're up walking around instead of sitting comfortably in front of the television. You've already seen me rant about how much time we spend in front of the television. Just do yourself a favor. Make a vow to yourself to go just a couple of hours with the television turned off. I know that's hard for some people. As soon as you hit the door, you click the TV on, and even if it's just for background noise, you have it on.

The problem is, again, it distracts you. It distracts you from getting important things done. So, turn it off. It's hard to be distracted by a big, old, black screen, and you may think you're going to go crazy as a result, but I promise you won't. In fact, you might end up getting a little work done. You might be able to exercise. You might be able to have a conversation with people in your family, or you might be able to read a book or do something that, again, makes you smarter, moves you closer to where you'd really like to be in life. But you have to remove some of the distractions, and one of the ways you do it is to turn the television off.

Just Stay Busy

Here's one last idea for getting more done: just stay busy. Don't always concern yourself with whether you're doing the right thing or whether it's moving you closer to your goals. That's important, but the most important thing is to stay busy all the time. Always make sure that you are doing something.

How will you know what's the right thing? Again, look at the results. If you're moving closer to where you'd like to be, then that activity was a good thing. If it didn't get you very far, or the result didn't matter that much, then dump it and don't worry about it. Don't do it anymore, but the key is stay busy. Build momentum. Momentum moves you along.

I've just given you some ideas on how you can get more done, but again, *how* doesn't matter. Take out a pen, put it to paper, and figure out *why* it's important to get more done.

Do you have goals that you can't reach because you think you're too busy? Do you have goals that you can't reach because you're tied up in activity instead of accomplishment? Do you have things that need to get done that you haven't been able to get done because you didn't have a strong enough reason to make sure they did? This is your opportunity to identify those things. Write them down and keep them with you so you'll have a strong motivation to make sure that you really do get more done.

Be Specific

I've already talked about the importance of setting and achieving goals and writing them down. I've done that a lot already in this book, but you can't emphasize it too much, because it is critical to your success. So I want to talk a bit more about how you can achieve more through goal setting and goal achievement. Remember, it doesn't matter to just set the goals. You have to actually accomplish them if you're going to move closer to where you want to be in life.

So do this. First of all, write your goals down. Duh. I say that about everything. Write them down. Know where you would like to be. Know what you want your life to look like in all its different areas. When you write down your goals, make sure that they're challenging. Don't make a plan that just leaves you with a mediocre life. Make a plan that challenges you and that's going to be fascinating to accomplish and that you're going to be so proud of once you've accomplished it. This means you have to have great, big goals—in every single area of your life, physical, mental, spiritual, financial, civic, family, career.

When you're writing these things down, you have to be specific. I work with a lot of people on money these days. When I say, "How many of you would like to have more money?" everybody says, "Oh yeah, I'd like to have more money." I pull a person out of the crowd and say, "Here's a quarter. Now you have more money. Go back to your chair, and be happy." They look at me like I'm an idiot. I say, "What are you upset about? You said you wanted money. I just gave you a quarter. You have more money. What are you complaining about? I don't understand." Everybody starts to chuckle at that point, but you can't just say, "I want more. I want more health. I want more money. I want more time." You have to be very specific. You have to know exactly what your goal looks like, smells like, tastes like. You have to know the address that you want to live at. You have to write down the area of town where you want to live.

Many years ago, I wasn't doing very well. I'd lost my company, I'd lost my business, filed bankruptcy, was on the way fighting to get my life back the way I wanted it to be, and I had some goals. At one point, I would drive through neighborhoods with my family and say, "This is where I want to live, right here, in this neighborhood."

Then one day my son was signed up to run in a race, so we drove to this other side of town, and it happened to be in the part of town where I said I eventually wanted to live, and I parked on the street in front of a big house. When I got out, it was a beautiful spring day. It was in front of this gorgeous house, and I said, "You know, guys, this is where I want to live. In fact, I want to live right here."

We walked down a few blocks. After the race, we all were looking around the neighborhood, and we said, "Yup, this is where we want to live, Dad." Everybody said, "This is it."

I didn't think anything about it, but what was amazing was two years later, I lived in that house, in the house that I parked in front of that day. I didn't realize for another year later that that was the house, but what I had done was write that down on a sheet of paper. I wrote down the streets that I wanted to live on, the area of town, the neighborhood. I would drive through that neighborhood so I could feel it, see it, smell it, know what it looked like so I could experience it so that when it came to pass, I would know that that was part of my goals.

That may sound a little ridiculous to you. Well, it may be ridiculous unless you've done it, so I want you to do it. Know what you want your goals to look like. Be very specific about it. Don't just say you want to lose weight. Write down exactly how much weight you want to lose. Write down exactly what size pants you want to wear, what size dress you want to wear. You need to be specific about all of these things. You can't just say, "I want to lose weight." How much? I want more money. Exactly how much? I want to make sure that I have money set aside for retirement. How much money? By when? In what format? What investments?

You have to know exactly what you want your goals to look like by being very specific when you write them down. You can fine-tune them as time goes on. Just because you write them down once doesn't mean they have to stay that way. You'll constantly be coming back to this list and making them even more specific as you go on.

It Has to Be *Your* Goal

Next, make sure that your goals are very personal. Here's what I have found out. You can't accomplish somebody else's goal. Guys, let me ask you this. When your wife says, "Honey, you need to lose ten pounds," how motivated are you? Probably not all that motivated. Just because she wants you to do it doesn't mean you're going to do it. When *you* look in the mirror and go, "Man, I need to lose ten pounds," that's when you're motivated, because now it's a personal goal. You know you don't look the way you should. You know you're heavier than you ought to be.

Just because somebody else has a goal for you, that doesn't mean you're going to accomplish that goal. It has to be *your* goal. People change when they want to change, not when someone else wants them to change.

I get emails every day, usually about money and finances. People are always quick to say, "Larry, my daughter or my aunt or my cousin has a huge financial problem. Larry, their spending is out of control. I've tried everything in the world to help them change. Can you help them change?"

My response is always the same: "I can't help anyone change." I told you that at the beginning of this book. I can't help you change. It's about you. It's about *self*-help. No one else can do it for you. Nobody can make you want to change, and nobody can set a goal for you that isn't yours. When it's important enough for you to get involved, that's when you will do it.

You have your goals, and you have them written down. They're specific, they're big, they're challenging. Now I want you to figure out what you need to learn. As I've already said, one big way to turn your life around is to recognize you have a problem, or a goal, and then get the education you need.

Write down some things you need to know, books you need to read, people you need to talk to. There's information out there that you don't have right now that can help you achieve that goal. Figure out what that information is. Once you have, get the information and start to learn it. You have to always be willing to take action, and one way of taking action is by getting the education and then stepping out and applying that education. Remember about application. You have to actually go to work on the information that you've learned.

Every little bit of effort you make has a payoff. How do you keep the courage to go forward? By making little, bitty steps, taking action in little, bitty ways, having small victories, small wins, because every bit of action will encourage you and put courage into you. That will give you the drive and the motivation and the momentum to keep after that goal until you accomplish it.

When you're setting your goals, you need to set a completion date. You need to have at least a target date in mind. That date may slip. It may come faster than you planned, and you may not be quite as far along as you would like to be. It's OK to change the target date as long as you're still moving toward the goal. Don't be too easy on yourself here. Don't let the date slide so far out that the goal becomes never-ending, but it's OK to slide that date forward as long as you're making movement, and you have momentum, and you're having small victories along the way until you eventually do accomplish your goal.

Goal-setting is not a hard task. It mostly takes a sheet of paper and a pen and writing down what you want, figuring out what you need to do and learn along the way, and then taking action. Mostly, it comes from believing that you can actually do it. You have to believe that you can accomplish this goal. If you write these things down and say to yourself, "There's no way I'm going to be able to do this," or if you tell one of your friends or your spouse, and they laugh and say, "Who do you think you are?" I'm not going to bet my money on the chance that you're going to get it done. You have to set aside all those people who doubt you. You have to set aside your own doubts, and you have to believe this can be done. It may be hard; it may be a lot of work. If it's hard and a lot of work, that just makes the winning that much better. So it's going to be hard, but you have to believe you can actually do it.

When you achieve your goal, it's time to cele-brate. Every achievement needs a celebration. But

I will warn you: a lot of people celebrate in exact contradiction to the goal they've just reached. People say, "My goal is to lose twenty pounds in the next four months." In four months, they've lost their twenty pounds, and they reward themselves by eating a pie. That's contradictory to the whole idea of their goal. It's contradictory to what they set out to do. Don't reward yourself in ways that will contradict what you've just done to get there. Instead make the celebration something that's meaningful and significant to you. If it's a huge goal, you may want to involve other people, but never skip the payoff. Sometimes it's important to set the celebration in advance so you can look toward it and let it be part of the motivation.

Goal setting and goal achievement really are a simple process. I encourage you to take out a pen right now, put it to paper, and start thinking about each one of the steps that I've just given you—not just about how you will go through this process, but about why it's important for you to do it.

Remember, 3 percent of people have written down specific goals. You want to be part of those 3 percent. Why? Because those 3 percent always accomplish more than the other 97 percent put together.

Be Even Smarter

There's an old line from motivational speaker Jim Rohn: "People would do better if they knew better." I totally agree. You have to be smarter than you are right now. You may be saying, "Larry, I'm a pretty smart guy." That may be the case, but it doesn't mean that you couldn't be even smarter. The more information we have to work with, the more education we get, the better. I'm not talking about going to school. I'm talking about regular, daily information intake that allows you to know more about a big variety of things, that will help you do more in life, become more in life. Every single area of your life will be affected by the amount of education that you have. You control that.

The best way to get more education is by reading. Sadly, that's not what people do. We spend a lot of time watching television. The average American spends more than twenty hours a week watching television. We spend less than two hours a week reading. Did you know that in 2017, 24 percent of Americans said they hadn't read a book in the past year? Come on. We need that information, yet we let it slide right by us.

There are some great books out there. But when you're reading a book, don't look for too much. Sometimes we say, "There's so much stuff in there, I was overwhelmed." The problem is that you don't want to get overwhelmed. You just want to get *whelmed*. I want you to get just enough information to be able to take that information and actually do something with it. When? Today.

You only need one good idea. When reading a book like this one, find one great idea that you can take action on today. After you've used that idea, you can come back and get another one, but the key is to get one great idea that you can take action on today. That's what you need to be looking for when you read a book. What one idea resonates with me at this moment so that I'm willing to work hard and put it to use today?

There's a lot of information out there, from a lot of reputable resources. It's everywhere. It's hard to turn anywhere and not find great information available. You can go on the Internet and get it. You can go in any bookstore. Universities have evening classes that cost practically nothing; some community colleges offer programs that don't cost a dime. You can even watch good television. I say a lot of bad things about television, but I'm not really knocking television; I'm knocking the amount of time we spend watching it. Believe me, I love to watch television; I just try to control what I'm watching.

There's great information out there. Luckily, now there are so many stations, and so many of them are filled with great ways to live your life better, cook more healthy ways, to learn about travel, science, history.

My son Tyler is not much of a reader, but he has an education that amazes me, because he watches television to learn things. He can't tell you who the winning person is on *American Idol* or anything about *Dancing with the Stars.* I doubt he even knows those shows exist, but he can tell you a lot about health and life and food and history and nature—all from watching high-quality, educational television. Television is not a total substitute for books like this, but it is a way to supplement your education.

The other way you can become smarter is to hang around smart people. How do you do that? Go where smart people hang out. Where do smart people hang out? You know where. They hang out at good places: bookstores and lectures and concerts.

Did you know that your income is likely to be an average of the incomes of your five closest friends? That's a fact. Think right now of your five closest friends and estimate what their incomes are. You don't have to pick up the phone and call them; you pretty much know what their incomes are. Add them up, average them out, and I'm betting you that yours is almost the same as theirs.

If you're disappointed by that number, you probably ought to dump those people and get some smarter friends. Smarter people tend to make more money. You want to make more money and hang around smarter people, but we tend to hang around people we're most comfortable with, and we're most comfortable with people who are like us.

Smart people hang around other smart people. Why would they want to hang around stupid people? They can't relate to them. That also applies to health. Fat people hang around sorry, fat people. Happy people hang around happy people; it's why they're happy. It's hard to be happy when you're hanging around angry, sad, whiny, boring people.

Get the picture? Figure out the kind of person you want to be, and hang around that kind of people. How do you do that? You find out where they are, and you find out what you have in common with them. Make sure that you have an education, so you'll be comfortable with them. It's not that hard.

Get out that sheet of paper again. Get out a pen. Write down why it's important for you to be smarter. This one ought to be simple: You'll make more money. You'll be healthier. You'll be more satisfied in your relationships. Take these ideas, build on them, make them more specific, and make them apply to your life. Write them down right now.

Breaking Down Problems

A lot of times people say, "Larry, I'd like to do more. I'd like to do all the things that you're talking about here, but you don't understand; I have problems." Good. I'm glad you have problems. It shows you're alive. It shows you're aware.

There are a lot of idiots out there that don't believe they have any problems. In fact, there are signs. You've seen these signs; they're everywhere. They're just dumb. They say, "I don't have problems. I only have opportunities." I used to work with a fellow manager who had a big sign like that in his office. Every time I'd say I had a problem, he'd say, "No, Larry. There are no problems. There are only opportunities." This guy was an idiot. He had opportunities; I had problems. The faster I realized it was a problem and tackled it as a problem, the quicker I got through the problem and got it solved.

Some problems are not opportunities. They're just problems. It's OK to have a problem. What isn't OK is to wallow in the problem or deny it. Denying it doesn't do anything but prolong it.

So first of all, realize you have a problem. If you come to me and say, "Larry, I have a problem," good for you. What are you going to do about it? That's really the question. In fact, that's always the question: what are you going to do about it? That can be the question even when something good happens. Good. I'm glad something great happened to you. What are you going to do about it? How are you going to capitalize on it? That's the question you ought to be asking yourself all the time.

So you have a problem. What are you going to do about it? First of all, understand that you have to break that problem down. Break it down into small pieces that you can tackle. Sometimes problems seem overwhelming because they're too big to deal with as a whole. You have to break them down into small, manageable pieces.

For instance, let's say you're in debt. Most people are in debt. Usually they have too much debt, and they say, "I want to get out of debt." You don't just get out of debt. You need to break it down into little pieces. Write down every single place where you are in debt, take one, and say, "I'm going to focus on that one credit-card bill until it's gone." Or you could focus on your mortgage. You say, "I'm going to put all my effort and all my energy and all my money into my mortgage so it'll become current."

Or you don't have any savings, and you say, "I have to have some savings," so for the next six months, you're going to really focus on savings. You're going to pay your bills and figure out away to set a little bit aside. That way you're not tackling the entire problem all at once. You're breaking it down into small, manageable pieces. That's how you do it. All accomplishment comes down to accomplishing little, bitty things along the way.

Sometimes our problems are so big, so overwhelming, that we don't know where to start. Get out a pen and paper, break the problem down into small pieces, and start tackling the pieces.

Another issue is that we tend to disasterize the problem. We say, "Do you know what might happen? What if? What if?" We end up playing "what if?" until a relatively small issue becomes a huge issue in our minds.

That's why I'm a big believer in writing the problem down. I've discovered that problems get smaller when you write them down. They're not nearly as scary. Writing down your problem will allow you to focus on the real issue. It won't let your mind go crazy and problem bigger than it really is. So always write your problem down, and then don't focus so much on the problem. Focus on what you're going to do about it. Focus on the solution. Focus on the action that you're going to take to get you past where you are right now to where you need to be.

Sometimes we're so focused on the problem that it's all we talk about. We tell people, everybody we meet, "Let me tell you my situation," and you pour out your soul about all the bad things going wrong. First of all, they don't care, so don't involve them. Unless they can help you with a solution, it doesn't matter.

If you are going to talk about the problem, talk about what you are doing to solve it. Again, you focus on accomplishment, not activity. You focus on the solution, not on the problem itself, and don't be afraid to ask for help. You have to do the work, but also realize that sometimes you don't have all the answers, so you have to ask other people who have already been through your situation to see what they did or what you might do. Then thank them for the advice and go to work.

The key to solving a problem is (1) realizing you have one; (2) being realistic about it (and you do that by writing it down); (3) breaking it down into manageable pieces; and (4) going to work on it.

You need to be able to solve problems. Why? Write that down. Get your sheet of paper out right now and write down why it would be helpful to use these tactics in solving your problems.

Make Way for Happiness

People tell me they want to be happy. I want to be happy, don't you? Of course you do. We all want to be happier. Right now everybody seems to be talking about how unhappy they are with the situations they're facing, and I know we're all facing a lot right now.

So figuring out a way to be happier is very important. The quickest way to become happier is just lighten up a little. Seriously, folks. I don't care what you have going on in your life; lighten up. You're not going to get out of this thing alive anyway, so you might as well enjoy yourself a little bit along the way.

Second thing, forget blame. We try so hard to blame other people for our issues. I've already talked about taking responsibility and said you don't get to blame others. This is also important in terms of happiness. You cannot be happy as long as you're constantly blaming someone else for what's going on in your life.

I know things aren't perfect. I'm not happy about a lot of the things that are going on. I disapprove, but if I focused on that all the time, I would go crazy. I can't blame those people for my situation. I'm a big believer in taking responsibility, so I have to realize that my situation is mine; it doesn't matter what's going on out there. The only thing that matters is what's going on in here with me, and I've discovered I cannot be happy if I'm always blaming someone else for my situation.

Stop blaming others. It will allow you to be happier, because it puts you in control of your situation. It doesn't allow you any excuses. It doesn't allow you to vent outside of yourself. It only allows you to go—where? Where I tell everybody to go every single time: back to the mirror so you can face yourself and deal with yourself.

Next, forget guilt. I know that's an amazing concept for a lot of people. I'm not a big believer in guilt. Guilt doesn't serve any purpose. You can't go back and change one thing. If you messed up, and we all do, here's a better idea: instead of feeling guilty about it, step up to the plate and apologize to the person that you hurt. Apologize for the mistake that you've made. Guilt won't make you feel any better. You'll only feel better when you make amends and then start to move forward. See how that can make such a big difference in your happiness? Guilt doesn't make you happy. But making amends, apologizing, saying you're sorry, and then moving past the mistake will make you happy.

Next is this: forget luck. We say about somebody else, "Oh, he's lucky." Luck is where opportunity and preparation come together. The problem is, most of us aren't very prepared, and we don't recognize opportunities, so we don't find ourselves being very lucky.

Here's an idea: become prepared for whatever might come about. That's why I talk about how you have to get smarter. You have to get more education in many areas of life, so you will recognize opportunities and know how to take advantage of them. That way you are creating your own luck.

Next is this: talk about creating. Create your own set of circumstances. If you don't like the way things are going, change the direction things are going in. You are in control. Refuse to accept your condition. Just say no to the way things are, and instead go work to create a new condition, a new set of circumstances in your life.

Then focus on what you need to do right now. We spend too much time worrying, and I've already talked about disasterizing our problems, about the things that have happened in the past and the things that might happen in the future. You create your future by taking care of your present. *Right now,* what could you do to make your life better? That's what will give you courage and keep away discouragement away. Focus on the activities that you can be doing right now to move you closer to your goals. That action will give you confidence, and that confidence will make you happier.

Here's another one, and this is a big one for me: you have to give up the constant need to be right. I like to be right. I don't think I'm alone in this one. I think a lot of us enjoy being right, but here's what I've learned about being right: I can fight my way into any situation and pretty much prove I'm right every single time. I can. I have that ability. I know how to argue and I enjoy a good battle, but I've learned to pick my battles.

Sometimes it just isn't worth the fight. It isn't worth going into battle, because no one ends up the winner. Yeah, I may be right, but I've hurt a lot of people along the way, and I haven't proved anything. So I've learned that I don't have to always be right in all situations. When you give up the constant need to be right, you'll end up much happier.

Next is this. You need to scope up. Let me tell you what that means. You need to give up pettiness. Does it really matter between you and your spouse whether the toothpaste tube gets squeezed in the middle or at the end? At a restaurant, when you're out with your friends and you're splitting up the check, does it really matter that you had the iced tea and that one had beer and the other one just drank water? That's petty. Don't be that way. Pettiness is really unattractive. Scope up.

You want to be happier? Try being healthier. It's amazing how those two things go together. It is hard to be happy when you're not healthy, when you don't feel good or you're depressed. When you feel good when you wake up every morning, when you go to bed every single night feeling good, without aches and pains, you're a lot more likely to be happy. Don't give me any excuses: "I'm getting old, or I'm getting this, or I did that." None of those things matter. You need to figure out a way to get healthy if you're going to be happy.

Here's another way to be happy: compliment others. It only takes a moment. You're saying, "Larry, that makes *them* happy; it doesn't make *me* happy." You're wrong. Complimenting others is a great way for you to feel better about who you are. It doesn't take but a second. Help other people to have a good day. It will in turn allow you to have a much better day.

The next way to be happier is to continue to learn. Never think that you're done. Read more. (You know I'm big on that.) Go to seminars. Go to lectures. Watch good television. Go to museums. Travel a bit. Join a book club. Have great conversations with great people. Ask good questions. Continue to learn. There's always great information out there.

My mother is eighty-eight years old and blind, but she still learns things every single day. She calls me up and says, "Larry, did you know. . . ?" I say, "No, Mom, I didn't know that." I find it fascinating that at that age and in her condition, she's still constantly excited about learning new things.

Then rise above the approval of others. Man, I like this one. I saw it a long time ago; I think it was the title of a book: "What you think of me is none of my business." I like that line. I don't care so much about what other people think of me. Yes, it's somewhat important, but it's not that big a deal. What I think about myself is much more important. If I feel good about who I am, what I've said, what I've done, that is the most important thing to me. I don't live and die on the approval of other people. I think it's sad when people need other people's approval so much that they can't be happy without it. You must learn to rise above the approval of other people.

Next, fill your life with activities that you really enjoy. I know that's hard to do when you feel that all you have time for is work, work, work, but there also comes a time to play. You have to figure out something you can do at least once every day that you really enjoy doing, and then expand on that time as you can. Don't forget to play. You're going to be much happier. There's always time to play for just a few minutes. You can do something that you really like: cook a meal, make a sandwich, watch a little TV (if you keep it under control), read a book before you go to bed at night, get a little alone time, go for a walk. Do something that you enjoy, no matter how busy you are doing other things. Find something you can have fun doing, and do it once every day.

Then you need to learn how to relax. You know it doesn't take long to relax. You can figure out a way to relax just a couple of minutes a day if you learn techniques to quiet your mind and step away from all of the activity and the busyness and the things that clutter our minds. If you figure out a way to step away and learn how to relax, you're going to learn how to be a lot happier.

Here's a big one, and I hear it a lot: people say they're stressed out. You've probably said that before. "Oh my goodness, Larry, I'm so stressed out. No wonder I'm not doing any better than I am. I have so much stress in my life." They end up doing stupid things like going to stress-management classes. I have friends who teach stress management. Here's my question: why would you want to learn how to manage something that you don't want at all? What are you going to do—organize your stress? You want to get rid of your stress.

How do you do that? First, determine the cause of the stress. I believe stress comes from knowing what is right and then doing what is wrong.

Do this quick exercise for me. You can do this one mentally. You don't have to write anything down; this is a fast one. Just think of the one, single thing in your life that is causing you the most stress. That shouldn't take long. It should come to mind immediately, whether it be your finances, your boss, your spouse—you name it. You know the thing in your life that's causing you the most stress.

Got it? Of course you do. Here's the deal: you know what you ought to do about that. Yes, you do. Don't argue with me. You know exactly what you ought to be doing about that situation. You know the action you ought to take. You know what you need to say. You know what you need to do.

You see, it's not that thing at all that is causing you the stress. The stress is being caused because you're not doing what you know you need to do. Again, stress comes from knowing what's right— and you do know what the right thing is—and then doing what's wrong. Usually we get caught up in doing what's wrong, which is doing nothing at all.

You have to be willing to do whatever it takes to fix this thing. Take a minute right now to think about or jot down what you know you should do about the one thing that causes the most stress in your life. What should you do? What have you been doing? Maybe nothing, maybe just the opposite of what you should have been doing. That's what's causing you the stress.

If you want to remove the stress, take action. Do what you know is the right thing to do. That's really the key. The key is not that we have things that cause us stress. The key is that we don't do what we know we should do about it.

So here's what I suggest. Once you realize what is causing the most stress, go out and do what you know in your gut and in your heart and in your mind is the right thing to do. That's how you will relieve stress in your life: by taking action, by feeling the confidence that comes from getting past what's causing you stress and from moving you closer to where you want to be

You know what you ought to do. Don't tell me that you don't. I know you do. Now just go out and do it.

Here's a big one too. You have to master the ability to forgive others. You know, you can't be happy when you harbor ill will or hard feelings in your heart. You just can't. You can't be angry with someone and really be happy.

Here's an idea: get over it. I know it's hard, but just get over it. How do you do it? I don't know how you do it. It's hard for me sometimes. I don't care how you do it. That's right. I don't care. The important thing is to forgive others.

Remember this: when you give someone a piece of your mind, you've given up your peace of mind. I heard that line a long, long time ago, from my mom. My peace of mind is very important to me, and I can't have peace of mind as long as I'm unwilling to forgive others for little things they've done to me. I've also learned over time that I pretty much forget them anyway, so I might as well go ahead and forgive them now. I won't remember them in a few months.

Then be generous. That's right. Be generous. It's amazing how just being a little charitable with your time and your money and the stuff that you have will make you feel much better. Learn to share. It's a great concept for being happy.

Then, enjoy the money that you have in any way you want. Here's my rule about money. Save 10 percent, invest 10 percent, be charitable with 10 percent, and figure out how to enjoy the rest. One thing is pay all your obligations. I like having my bills paid, so that makes me happy, but after you've done all those things, you do get to enjoy your money. That doesn't mean you go out and buy things you can't afford. In fact, it means just the opposite. Make sure you have enough money to afford the things that you enjoy. It's a great way to make sure that you're happy.

Here's the big one if you want to live a happier life. Don't overlook this one; this is probably the most important step for being happy. Don't look for things outside of yourself to make you happy. Happiness comes from within. Way too often, we look for things outside of ourselves. Some people like to shop, some people eat. Some people both eat and shop. They're overweight, but they dress really cute.

Nothing outside of yourself is ever going to bring you true, internal happiness. Happiness is an inside job, and when we realize that and stop constantly looking for other things to make us happy, then we will figure out what it takes to really make us happy. So don't be looking for external things to bring you internal happiness. Figure out what makes you happy from the inside out.

I want you to sit down right now and figure out the things that really make you happy. Then determine *why* those things make you happy. Do a little self-analysis here. Then think about all the things outside of yourself that you believe make you happy.

Identify those, and ask yourself some tough questions: do these things make me happy, or am I kidding myself? This is a great time to figure out what in your life does make you happy, what doesn't make you happy, how you've been fooling yourself, and what action you can take to make sure you're living a happier life. Take a few moments now with a pen and a sheet of paper.

Random Pointers

Here are some random thoughts on some short things that all of us could do to live a happier, better life.

First of all, to get started, just start. Don't complicate it any more than that. Just start. I don't care how, I don't care what your excuse is, just start. You want to quit smoking? Stop putting cigarettes in your mouth.

Here's how to deal with criticism. Don't. Rise above the constant need for approval from others.

Here's how to have a positive attitude: don't bother. Yup, that's right. Don't bother. A positive attitude won't make you any more successful anyway. In fact, I'm a big believer in having a negative attitude. You won't hear many people say that. Whey do I say have a negative attitude? Sometimes you have to get negative about the things in your life so you can go out and take positive action in your life. You will create positive results when you get a little fed up, a little negative about the way you've been living, about the way you've been spending, about the way you've been eating, about the way you've been treating and talking to others. So get a little negative sometimes in order to create positive results.

You want to know how to avoid problems? You can't. Problems are just a part of life. The only people without problems are dead people.

Here's how you get others to change: you can't. People change when they want to do, not when you want them to.

You want to win every single argument? You can't. You can't win every argument. Sometimes you're going to lose. It happens. Deal with it. Besides, about half the arguments you get into, you deserve to lose. Why? You're wrong. There are other arguments that you should never have gotten into to begin with, and it doesn't matter whether you win or lose. Just win the ones that count.

Here's my last one. You want to know how to age gracefully? Let me ask you a question: why would you want to do that? Go out kicking and screaming. Old age is not for sissies. Stay fit, stay fun, and kick ass until you die.

How We Can Create a Better World

I've given you a lot of things that you can act on, and hopefully, I've asked you some questions that you can think seriously about. I want to close this off by giving you a list of things that I think we should all do to create a better world. We all want a better world. Let's talk about how you actually do this. These are pretty simple, and I have some very simple ideas that if all of us followed these, it would create a better world.

1. Love more and hate less. I know that sounds like a silly, airy-fairy idea, but we do. Just hate less. We need to love folks more, and we need to show that love through our money and through our actions and through our time and how we live our lives.

2. Recycle. We only have one planet. We need to take care of it, and one of the ways we take care of it better is by recycling.

3. Become more involved. Don't just be a spectator of life. Don't watch life go by. We need to become involved in every single area of life that matters to us.

4. Support organizations that feed and clothe those who really need it. I'm not a big believer in bailouts or handouts, but I know there are people in this world who need help. I'm not talking about those who won't take care of themselves; I'm talking about people who *can't* take care of themselves, people who have been through horrible tragedies—hurricanes, disasters. There are lots of people in this world who need our help, and we need to support the qualified organizations who help them.

5. Don't litter. Yeah, I'm a big believer in that. Don't throw your crap on the ground. We have trash cans; we have trash bags. Don't throw stuff on the ground. It may sound like a little deal to you. It's a big deal to me, and I think it's a big deal to a lot of other people.

6. Do something every single day to help another person smile. Make somebody happy. Compliment them. Hold the door open for them. Be nice to them.

7. Buy things from little kids. Yup, little kids still knocking on the door selling candy bars or magazines to raise money for their school

events. Little kids need our help, and they need encouragement, and they need some experience and entrepreneurism.

Because You Can

I guess here's what it really all comes down to: Why should you do all this? Why should you go through the effort and the heartaches and the headache and break a sweat to change your life? Why should you want to work so hard to make these lists and change your life? You're doing pretty good. Pretty good might be all right with you. Pretty good is not all right with me. I want more. I believe that deep down, we all want more. Why should you want more? Why should you want to earn more money, be healthier, have better relationships? Why should you want to stop the way you're living right now and figure out a way to live better? Why would you want to take my advice in this book?

I used to ask myself that. I've been a student of self-help and personal development for a good, long while. Here's what it all comes down to. You should do the things that I'm talking about here because of three basic words: *because you can.*

You can do more, and if you can do more, you ought to do it. If you could give more, if you could work harder, if you could be better at what you do, if you could be nicer, if you could be smarter, if you could be richer, healthier, if you could be all those things, and I honestly believe that you can, then you ought to—simply because you can.

That ought to be enough for you. You do everything you can because you can. I want to remind you that you can do whatever you decide to do if you're willing to work hard enough to make it happen. You can have the life that in the past you've only dreamed of. You can actually make come about the things that you said that you wanted but were never able to accomplish, because your actions were contradictory to your words.

Now I want you, maybe for the first time, to align your actions with your words so you start to make a positive change and create better results in your life. Why should you do it? Remind yourself of this every single day: you should do it because you can.

4

Fix the World by Fixing Yourself

All right, folks, now let's just freewheel it through some things that I believe are important for all us to know. There's a lot of frustration right now in society. People have a lot of questions. I go on television, usually a couple of times a week, to talk about all the things that are going on in society. People turn to me, and I think it's because I give straight talk. You may not agree with where I am politically. You may not agree with a lot of what I say here, but at least I believe in what I have to say, so take a few minutes here and read my rant about some of what's going on.

How We Got out of Control

One question I get is, "Larry, how did we get so out of control? How did we wind up in the mess that we're in? Why are things the way they are?"

My answer is, "How can we be surprised that things aren't even worse?" We haven't been paying attention for a good, long while. The fact is that 21 percent of the people who could vote in America aren't even registered to vote, and typically only half of the people who are registered to vote actually go to the polls. We don't care enough about our government is concerned, about who the president is or who our congressmen are. We don't care enough about those things to actually go to the polls and vote. We're quick to complain, but we're not involved in the process. I say that it's our fault we have the current mess because we didn't care enough to end up with anything else.

We hold everybody else to a standard we don't hold ourselves to. We have people right now in our country saying, "That's not fair. We have congressman who are cheating on their taxes." Well, isn't that unfair. How dare they? But the reality is that 25 percent of all of us cheat on our taxes, yet we don't want anybody else to do that. We're living a double standard. We're kidding ourselves. We're lying to ourselves.

You can carry that over to parenting. We look at our kids and say, "We want you to be honest and to have integrity," and yet a fourth of us cheat on our taxes. We're not living that. We're not setting that up as a role model. We're not showing our kids that's how they ought to live their lives or spend their money.

We expect of others what we don't expect of ourselves. The reason we're in this mess right now is that we simply didn't care enough not to get in this mess. We didn't become involved in our government. We didn't expect the best from our elected officials because most of us didn't even vote to elect them. We just want to sit back and complain about them. We got in this mess because we weren't involved.

You see, that's personal responsibility. I told you I'm the pit bull of personal development based on that one concept: taking personal responsibility. We all need to take personal responsibility, and the problems we have now—economic problems, parenting problems, problems with our government— all come down to the fact that we stopped taking personal responsibility, and we left it up to somebody else.

You know what I've discovered? Nobody can take care of my money like I can take care of my money. Nobody can take care of my family like I can take care of my family. Nobody will raise my kids the way I want them raised except me. It's up to me. No one can pay my bills except me. No one ought to pay my bills except me. It's always up to me.

I used to do wealth seminars around the country. I stopped doing them because I think most of them right now are a sham. There are people on the program saying how to become a millionaire the quick and easy way.

I recently did one of those. I followed a man who had said this onstage and said, "You've just listened to a man lie to you for the last hour, because no one gets to be a millionaire quick and easy. Every millionaire I know got there the slow and hard way: by working every single day harder than anybody else was willing to work."

The key is this: what are you doing today? Ask that of yourself. What am I going to do today that moves me a little closer to where I really want to be? That's it. You're trying to fix the whole world. Why don't you fix yourself? That's what it comes down to. What am I going to do that makes my family better?

Tend Your Own Garden

I was recently asked about the economy: "Larry, how do you feel about this, and how do you feel about that?" I said, "I don't feel any way about any of that stuff. It doesn't matter to me. I can't control those things." The only thing I can do every day is go home and take care of my house, take care of my family, take care of my own personal economy. It doesn't do any good to whine, complain, and moan about everything that's going on if I can't do anything about it.

What do I do instead? I take control of my life, and that's what I suggest everybody do. Take control of your own personal life. Ask yourself, "What can I do today to make my life a little better? What can I do today to improve my personal economy? What can I do today to make sure that my bills are paid?" When you take care of your personal economy, you make sure your bills are paid. You're taking care of your house. If we all do that, then everything gets better for all of us. We fix the whole by fixing the parts of the whole, and you are one of those parts. If you want to fix the government, if you want to fix the economy, if you want to fix the way the world works, then fix the way *your* world works. That's how it is.

Here's another thing. I go on shows with people who say, "Larry, here's one of the big keys to success. We just have to stay positive in this time of trouble." Let me tell you, folks, staying positive is probably a waste of time. I think you're going to have to get negative to get ahead in this situation. I think we have to get negative about the way things are. I think we have to get fed up. I think we have to argue and complain, and I think it's important for us to get fed up, and then take action on the fact that we're fed up.

Sometimes you have to get negative in order to take positive action and create positive results. We have all those self-help people out there who are talking about the power of a positive attitude. They're out there saying, "Just put on your rose-colored glasses, and dust off your old smiley-face button, and plaster a big, fake smile on your face." It could make me puke. Let me ask you: how's that stuff working for you?

Then we hear those people say, "Whatever the mind can conceive and believe, it can achieve." What if your mind can't conceive anything? What if you believe you're an idiot? What are you going to achieve then? Here's my idea. I think you have to look at the way things are, get ticked off about the way things are in your life and in our country and in the world and take action. You take action by voting differently. You take action by looking at your life and saying, "Holy crap, I'm sick of living this way. I deserve better than this."

You need to surround yourself with friends, I mean real friends who look at you and say, "Are you kidding me? You're going to put up with your life the way it is?" Don't find one of those friends who's going to put their arm around you, hold your hand, say, "Let's just sing 'Kumbaya' together while we roast marshmallows and make s'mores." That doesn't make your life better.

If you want your life to get better, get a little negative about it. It's OK to get a little negative. Get a little negative so you know you're better than this. You deserve better than this. Our country deserves better than this.

So now we're going to become involved. We're going to not just be spectators in our own lives or in the life of our country and the lives of our communities. We're going to speak up. We're going to do what's right, think what's right, and take action on what's right. If you want to turn things around in your own life, if you want to turn things around in your business, in your community, and in our country, you will stop being so passive. You will stop being so full of positive ideas, and you will get realistic to the point where you will create positive results by understanding that a negative situation needs action.

So it's OK to get a little negative and then take positive action that will produce some positive results. That's our challenge—creating positive results.

Make Some Changes

Here's another one. It's real popular: change. Did you know that the most popular topic for any platform in the world today is change? More people are writing books and giving speeches about change than about any other thing.

Change. The whole topic amazes me. Change has been around for a pretty good long while, and we act like it's a brand-new concept. Every group I speak to always says, "We have to make sure Larry understands that we're going through a lot of change." Duh.

I'm going through a lot of change. You're going through a lot of change. What amazes me is that change bothers people as much as it does. The very idea of telling someone that they have to change their routines, their habits, just makes their little hearts beat so hard. That's usually because they're so comfortable in the rut they've dug that even if they're headed down the wrong path, they're going to stay on it simply because it doesn't involve any change. What are you afraid of? Make some changes.

I've watched people sit in a room that they absolutely hate because they don't have the energy or the inclination to change the furniture around or buy a gallon of paint and paint the room. People are afraid to look in the mirror or step on the scale because they know they're overweight and in order to get control of their life, they'd have to change their lifestyle.

I talk to people who've spent way too much money, and I say, "Let me tell you how to fix that. You have to adjust your lifestyle."

They go, "What? Adjust my lifestyle? Change? I can't change. I'm comfortable with the way things are."

People are comfortable with their lives; otherwise they'd change their lives. It works that way in every area. I don't understand it. Personally, I like change. I move all the time. I move offices every couple of years at least. I change houses every three or four years. I like to move. I like the change. It allows me to clear out the clutter of my past few years. It clears out my mind when I make a change in my business. It keeps me creative, it keeps me fresh, it keeps me on the edge. That's what happens when we have changes.

Change is usually a great opportunity for all of us if we learn how to take advantage of it. The problem is most people won't change even when they know they should. Why? Again, it's usually because they're comfortable. Sometimes they're just afraid.

Feel the Fear

Many years ago, I read a great book by Susan Jeffers. It was called *Feel the Fear and Do It Anyway.* What a great title: *Feel the Fear and Do It Anyway.* Read the book if you can, but right now just think about the title. You're going to be afraid from time to time. It happens. There's no way around it. It happens to me. Yes, it even happens to me. Sometimes I'm afraid. Hard to believe, but I am.

I did a show on CNBC called *The Millionaire Inside.* It was hilarious. I was watching television one night, and they ran a commercial for the show. It said, "Watch CNBC's *The Millionaire Inside,* with four of the world's leading money mentors." Then it named them all. I was one of them. I was amazed: suddenly I was one of the world's leading money mentors.

When I was shooting this show in New York City, I was in the green room with Jennifer Openshaw and David Bach and Robert Kiyosaki and Keith

Ferrazzi. I have to admit I felt some fear. I'm totally confident when I go on stage, but suddenly I was going to be on national television, to be aired maybe 100 times, and I had to be able to hold my own with renowned experts on money.

Now I was afraid, I will admit, yet I walked out on that stage with confidence. I grabbed a stool and a microphone, and I did pretty well. In fact, looking back at it, I was pretty amazing. Did it mean I wasn't afraid? No, I was afraid, but I had confidence in my ability, and I had the desire to win no matter what. I felt the fear, but I did it anyway.

Often I'm afraid of what I have to do. I'm even more afraid of not doing it. That's really the key: I'm afraid not to do it. I impose my own consequences. I'm a big believer in consequences. As I've said, I believe that we ought to feel the pain of the consequences.

Sometimes I create my own negative consequence. What do I do? I have to understand first of all that every action has a consequence, but every nonaction has a consequence too. So in my life, I create my own consequences regardless of whether I take the action or don't take the action, and this is the consequence I create: personal disappointment.

I don't want to let myself down. I set a high standard for myself, so I'm disappointed in myself when

I've done less than my best. I'm not looking to be *the* best; I just want to do *my* best, and I know what my best is. Other people don't know what my best is; only I do. That's my standard. I learned a long time ago that people don't know what I'm doing really well. Only *I* know what I'm doing really well.

Sometimes I give speeches. I walk off the stage, and I know that on a scale of one to ten, that day I had been a four. Yet the audience leaps to their feet for a standing ovation. I've also gone onstage and known that on a scale of one to ten, I was probably a fifteen that day, and they looked at me like a dog looking at a ceiling fan. They didn't get it. They just sat there in their chairs.

After twenty years of going on stages around this world, speaking to all kinds of groups, I realized that audiences don't know a good speech from a bad speech. It doesn't matter, though. *I* know the difference between a good speech and bad speech. *I* know whether I've done my best or not. My goal is always to do my best, so I set up that kind of consequence for myself.

When we do things that challenge us, it's not the fact that we make mistakes or that we don't do well that really matters. What matters is that we never tried, that we didn't deal with what we were handed.

Right now, you're going to have to change the way you have been doing things. You're not going to be able to act the way you have in the past, because every aspect of our environment is changing right now. How we do business is changing. We have to work harder than we have in the past. It takes more to serve people well than it did in the past. It means that you have to go to work every single day and work harder to keep your job than you did in the past. It means that you have to actually be able to pay people back before they give you the credit. Our credit standards are going up. It means that you have to keep your word more than ever before. You have to be a better person. You have to be a smarter person, because there are more people in the job market out there who want your job and may be more qualified than you.

You're going to have to learn more, which means you have to change everything about the way you live your life. You can gripe about it, whine about it, moan about it, but it doesn't matter. Change is upon us. You'd better welcome it. You'd better roll with it. You need to understand that no one cares what you're going through. We all have excuses for not doing well. Today no excuse is going to fly.

You have to do whatever it takes that's legal, moral, and ethical that allows you to be the very best in who you are and what you do, because this is a tough environment out there. We're all in it, and it means you have to change in order to survive. Embrace it, enjoy it, go with it, and take advantage of it.

You know what I've discovered? Nothing works anymore. That's right. Nothing works.

Things Don't Work

Government doesn't work. That can't come as a surprise to you, and it doesn't matter what party you're in right now. I'm not going to talk about Democrats or Republicans or Libertarians or Independents. It doesn't matter. We know that. Sadly, it just doesn't work right now.

Health care doesn't work. People are dying and being denied health care simply because they don't have any money. Here we are: we live in the richest, best country in the world. Really? Yet we're letting our citizens die because they can't afford insurance or medicine.

Insurance doesn't work. You fight to get them to pay for everything they promised they would pay for to begin with, and then if you fight and win, they'll cancel you after they pay your claim. Sadly, most elderly people can't afford their own medicine.

There's something wrong with that, folks. Health care doesn't work. Insurance doesn't work.

Our public-school system doesn't work. Our kids are so far down the list in math and science by comparison to other countries that we ought to be ashamed. We have kids who walk out of their high schools with a diploma in their hand, and they can't even read it.

Teachers are allowed to keep their jobs even after they make racist remarks and sexual advances on our children. Why? Because they have tenure. That's despicable. We ought to fire teachers because they're incompetent. How do you determine whether a teacher is incompetent? When they turn out kids who are stupid and can't read and can't add and can't subtract and don't know what the teachers are supposed to be teaching them.

I know that fires people up. Not long ago I wrote this in a blog, and a teacher wrote me and said, "That's not fair. You can't judge teachers based on how well their students do." Oh, really? I judge salespeople by whether they make sales or not. I judge managers by whether their employees do what they're hired to do or not. I ought to be able to judge teachers by whether their students learn what they're supposed to learn or not. So proof again: the public-school system doesn't work.

How does all this happen? I don't know. Products don't work. Clothes don't last. You buy a new computer—I bought a new computer. It lasted about two years. I wanted to get it fixed. It cost more to fix my two-year-old computer than it did to buy a new one. I think that's called planned obsolescence. As a result of that idea, I have five computers in the closet, because it cost me more to fix them—and they weren't major fixes—than it did to buy a new replacement. Our clothes don't last anymore. Basically, anything we buy doesn't last. Why is that?

People don't work very hard either. For the most part, people just work hard enough so they won't get fired. Typically, companies pay them just enough so they won't quit, and I'm sick of listening to people tell us that Americans are the hardest-working people on the planet. Get honest, people. That's not the truth.

Politicians love to tell us that. They love to blow smoke up our skirt and say America has the hardest-working people on the planet. That's a load of crap, folks. American workers are not the hardest-working people on the planet. Read a little bit. Watch some educational television. Travel some. You're going to quickly find out that that is not true. We are lazy people who, for the most part, work just hard enough to squeeze by.

You tell one of your employees that you're upset with the fact they're not working very hard and you're tired of the crappy job they're doing. They're probably going to contact their union rep and file a grievance because you had the audacity to attack their performance.

I'm still from the old school. You get paid for working. If you don't work, I have the right to fire you, and you don't have the right to complain about it. The reality is that people don't work very hard anymore. The average American is not doing their job.

The average American typically is overweight. Sorry: that's the way it is; the average American is overweight. Nationwide, we have an obesity rate of 40 percent.

The average American is not very well educated. They read on a seventh-grade level if they read at all. Typically, we're broke. The average fifty-year-old only has $2,500 saved; 50 percent of our society spends more money than they earn. The average credit-card user has nearly $5,500 in credit-card debt right now.

So don't tell me that we're the most fascinating, amazing, best people on the planet when we're overweight, undereducated, and underdisciplined, and when we're not working as hard as we're supposed to work. In fact a recent study said the average American actually works only about 50 percent of the time they're on the job. They admitted to that.

Come on. If we want to get ahead, if we want to fix things, we have to go back to the basics, and the basics are this: We have to do the right thing no matter what, regardless of what the situation is. We have to do the ethical thing, which means the right thing. We have to do what we said we would do, when we said we would do it, the way we said we would do it. That's how we have to live our lives. That's how we have to raise our kids. That's what we have to do in our relationships. That's what we have to do in our businesses. That's how we have to treat our customers and our employees and our employers. It all comes down to a matter of ethics and morality and justice and integrity.

The basics of life are really very simple. We have gotten away from those, and that's one reason nothing works the way it's supposed to. We have an excuse for everything. There is no excuse. Get back to the basics, folks. The reason nothing works right now is because so few of us work.

There are a lot of negative things going on right now, but the bottom line is that people are saving more than they did in the past, because after the last ten years, they realize that you'd better have some cash on hand.

I was recently on a program with a bunch of financial people. They said, "This is going to happen; that's going to happen." They turned to me and said, "Larry, what's your take on all of this?"

"I don't care what all of us are saying right now," I said. "It's nothing but speculation. Everything we say about what might happen with the economy is speculation. We don't know."

When it comes to money, this is all we know: (1) You ought to pay your bills because you said you would. Period. (2) If something bad happens—and you can't count on that not being the case in your life—you'd better have some cash on hand, because cash can fix just about anything. It may not be able to make it right, but it sure can make it better. You better have some cash on hand, so one of the good things to come out of all this bad is that for the first time in a long time, people are actually starting to save.

Another good thing is that people are starting to understand how our overall economy works. I recently did a call-in program called *Your Money, Your Questions.* One of the questions was, "Larry, how do you feel about the fact that the Dow dropped 180 points yesterday?"

I said, "Do you know what the Dow is?"

"No."

"Do you have any money in the stock market?"

"Not really."

"Then why are you worried about it?" I said. "Why do you care that the Dow dropped 180 points yesterday? You don't even know what that means, and you don't have any money in the stock market. Don't worry about it."

For the first time, people are starting to learn what those things mean. They're starting to become aware.

When overall, you look at all the bad things that are going on right now, some good is going to come out of it. It's allowing us to take control of our situation, economically, from a government standpoint, and in every single area of our lives. We can start to make real headway about the things that are affecting our lives, and we'll change the world when we change us.

Fixing Our Society

You have to admit it: health care is a problem. I've been on a rant about health care in a lot of different ways, but instead of trying to fix the health care system, why don't we reduce our need for health care? Seems to me like that's a better idea.

We're throwing money at something to fix sick people. Why don't we teach people not to get so sick? Doesn't that make sense? So let's attack health care issues at the real source of the problem, which is illness.

The top two causes of illness in America right now are obesity and smoking. If that's the case—and it is, you can check me—let's incentivize people to lose weight and stop smoking. We would reduce our need for health care, and we would become a healthier society in the process. To do that, we ought to add a $5 tax on every pack of cigarettes. We could call that an idiot tax. If you're going to buy a pack of cigarettes for $5, we're going to charge you an added $5 worth of tax. Some people would say that wouldn't stop people from smoking. I understand that, but it'd make it hurt a little bit more. Sometimes we need to add to the pain of people making stupid decisions.

In conjunction with that, I was recently on a television show where they were for locking in interest rates on credit cards at 15 percent. They asked me my opinion on that. I said, "I think we ought to raise interest rates on credit cards to 75 percent." Everybody was aghast. They said, "Why would you want to do that, Larry?"

I said, "I want people to reach for their credit card and think long and hard before they pull it out. I want it to become so painful for them to use their credit cards that they have to think long and hard. I want them to really think about whether they really need to buy that bottle of pop or that pack of gum when they're getting their gasoline. I want it to hurt when they use their credit cards. That's why I think we ought to raise the percentage to 75 percent interest on use of a credit card."

I think we ought to give tax breaks for any and all education. Our society is simply not as smart as it ought to be. We make bad decisions, personally, professionally, and financially many times simply because we're uninformed. We aren't as smart as we should be. Again, it goes back to that old line, "If we knew better, we would do better." So offer a tax break based on the amount of money you spend on any type of education. That could be formal education, but it could also be for seminars and books and educational. Anything that allows you to be smarter gives you a tax break. Can you imagine that? You buy a book by Larry Winget, you get a tax break for doing it. How cool is that?

That's it. It's really that simple. You reward people for good behavior—becoming healthier, getting a better education. That's positive performance, and I want to reward people for doing the right thing as a reminder to the next generation that we reward good performance, not bad performance. If you make a mistake, we're not going to be there to bail you out. If you do the right thing, we're going to help you make that decision to continue to do the right thing. See how simple it is? Why haven't we done this? I don't know.

All right, folks, we're to the end. By now you may be saying, "Man, this is really all pretty simple." You see, that's the problem with my message. It is simple. I try to take away all of the excuses you've used in the past.

Ultimately that's not what people really want. They don't want it to be simple. They want it to be hard, because if they buy into the idea that it's hard, they will have an excuse for not doing well, and I simply don't believe there is an excuse for not doing well. Everybody has the ability to do well. You may not be able to fix every problem you have, but you can have a positive impact on every problem you have by doing a few simple things. You can make your situation better than it is right now.

That's my message. Take a few simple ideas, put them to work, and watch your life get better. Pick an area of your life. Don't complicate it by trying to attack everything at once. Just pick one area of your life that you want to attack and that you want to make better, and study some of the simple ideas that I've given you here. Make a list of why it's important for you to make your life better in that area, and then go to work. If you're going to learn one thing from this book, it should be to keep a pad of paper and a pencil at hand so you can write your ideas down.

If you try some of these very simple ideas in the area of your life that you feel needs the most work, I'll guarantee that you'll see a difference. Simple ideas with a simple action plan and a commitment to making a change is all that it takes for you to live a better life, and I believe that's what you really want. I honestly wish you the very best.

Printed in the USA
CPSIA information can be obtained
at www.ICGtesting.com
JSHW012033140824
68134JS00033B/3033

9 781722 502331